JOHN MARIN

JOHN MARIN

By MacKinley Helm

Kennedy Graphics, Inc. • Da Capo Press
New York • 1970

This edition of *John Marin* is an unabridged republication of the first edition published in Boston in 1948. It is reprinted by special arrangement with Mrs. Frances H. Helm.

Library of Congress Catalog Card Number 75-87484

SBN 306-71489-2

Copyright 1948 by Institute of Contemporary Art, Boston

Published by Da Capo Press
A Division of Plenum Publishing Corporation
227 West 17th Street, New York, N.Y. 10011

JOHN MARIN

BOOKS BY MacKINLEY HELM

John Marin

by MACKINLEY HELM

with a foreword by John Marin

PELLEGRINI & CUDAHY in association with THE
INSTITUTE OF CONTEMPORARY ART, BOSTON

ACKNOWLEDGMENTS

Grateful acknowledgment is made to Mr. John Marin for permission to quote from his letters and papers, published and unpublished; to Mrs. Dorothy Norman for providing the author with copies of unpublished letters from John Marin to Alfred Stieglitz; and to The Atlantic Monthly Company for permission to draw material from "John Marin: An *Atlantic* Portrait," by MacKinley Helm, published in *The Atlantic Monthly*.

MacKinley Helm

TO MY WIFE

Foreword

In the leaves of this book will be found
The goings on of this—
        critter myself—and reproductions of some of his playings—
        Sympathetically gathered and put down by one who believes
in this—critter myself—
        If you like what you read and what you see—all very well—
if you don't—well you just don't—
        but don't blame too much the one who has fused
this all together—a pretty good fusing—I'll say—and—with Style—
and plenty of careful labor. So—if you must blame him—blame him
for the Subject he chose—again—this Critter myself
        as to the why of the above Scribbling—well—
you see—I was asked to shove in a few leaves
        maybe what I say will spoil the book for I have
a Spleen—have a grouch to get off—my chest—
        anyway here goes
In the first place—having had a few physical and mental disturbances
myself—I am a great believer in—Health—
        not that these disturbances of life do not play
a role—they must
        but—that they should predominate—why?—
        So Health is my credo—
Looked at—most trees in the forest appear moderately in health
        —Looked at mentally all trees—can be—made to
look diseased
        There's the—so called—abstractionist—the so called—
non objective approach
        quite too often—a disease approach
        or from another point of view—streamlined of all humanity
where an old fashioned human embrace is quickly nullified
by divorce
        Or where nudity of the Object is blatantly shown for
the specific purpose of making it the supreme—Commondenominator—

where nudity is shown to rob it—itself—of its
appeal—yes of its—old fashion—sex-appeal

that sensitive people have
The going out of one's way to be different
always a questionable refuge—when one has—nought to say
Cannot the artist be or better that he be—a
well balanced healthy individual
Of course—there have been those—will be those who
with their disease have given to the world—and will give
Something Vital
They are not those I speak against
but that—deadly—humorlacking—
that deadly—fun and play lacking
Those who would Start Symphonies early in life—
those who would Startle the world whose—ideal—
is the advertisement—
is the noise
Just suppose we look at man—he hasn't changed much in
his physical appearance in the last Two thousand Years—
How Come—he's now so different
How Come—he now has this hatred of all things Seen—
And taking its place a diseased mental seeing
How Come—A pleasure in torture
an Exaltation of torture
Has it a great moral lesson—?
and what the Hell have moral lessons or any other lessons to do
with Art
The Creative one has his seeings and his own way of
putting them down—
If he's healthy mankind will find it out
If he's diseased mankind will find that out too
--anyway--
The birds are still singing
—out there—

Contents

Plates

IN COLOR

IN BLACK AND WHITE

Colorplates A, B, C, F, G, H, by courtesy of Raymond & Raymond Galleries, New York; colorplate E courtesy of the Miller Company, Meriden, Connecticut; colorplates D and I courtesy of The Institute of Contemporary Art, Boston. Grateful acknowledgment is made to The Institute of Contemporary Art, Boston, and the Museum of Modern Art, New York City, for permission to reproduce the major portion of the black and white plates.

JOHN MARIN

The Long Boyhood

1870 — Spring, 1905

THE SINGLE MEMOIR OF JOHN MARIN'S FRENCH GRAND-
father, known as Jean-Baptiste Marin when he migrated from France with
his wife, is a faded letter in flowing script and colloquial English. Addressed
at Saratoga, New York, on August 25, 1853, it was written to Marin's father,
John Marin II, a well-grown boy who was spending the summer with a
younger brother in New York City, the winter home of their parents. Apart
from the contents of the letter, which suggest that the writer kept a summer
hotel at the Springs, Marin knows nothing about his paternal grandfather
except that his surname was Spanish, though he was christened in French;
and that he wore in his skull a round silver plate, a souvenir of the flight
of the *Grande Armée* from Moscow. This is the letter which survives among
Marin's papers:

Dear Son:
I received your letter but have not had time to answer it until
now. The people are leaving soon (?) and I am not so busy as I
have been. One of you can come up anytime you like. Get that
wood sawed up and have it all ready for winter. You need not ex-
pect us until about the 1st of October on account of the state fair
which commences the 20th of September and will last 4 days. Your
Mother has been unwell for two days but is now getting better.
My health is much better than it was and I am getting smart
again. If one of you come up soon bring me my agreement with
Mr. Daly. If you cannot come send it to me by mail soon. Give
my compliments to Mr. & Mrs. Sherry, etc.
Your affectionate Father,
John B. Marin

John Chéri Marin, to whom the letter was written, married Annie
Louise Currey of Weehawken, New Jersey, in Grove Church, New Durham
—now part of North Bergen—nearly fourteen years later, on April 9, 1867,
and took her home in a carriage to a large, pleasant house in Rutherford,
on the west side of the Hackensack Meadows. Approached by a tree-bordered
avenue which began at a gatehouse, the house was surrounded by lawns and

3

gardens whose shrubs and flowers were known to John Chéri Marin by their botanical names. Mrs. Marin—to judge from old portraits—had a patrician appearance, of which the most notable item, a Currey characteristic, was the high, flushed cheekbone under curly brown hair. She bore John Marin III on December 23, 1870, and died nine days later, the first day of January in the following year. Marin's father straightway drove his pair eastward, across the Hackensack Meadows, and left his son in Weehawken with his grandfather and grandmother Currey, who, with their maiden daughters, Jenny and Lelia, and their son, Richard Currey, were great Bible readers of Yankee descent. And with those pious kinsmen Marin grew up to be as frugal and plain as themselves, in his life and his painting.

John, the first American Currey, Marin's Yankee ancestor, came from Leeds, in the West Riding of Yorkshire, and settled in Peekskill, New York, in 1700. There was a family tradition—it found its way into the death notices of Miss Lelia Currey in the Union Hill papers in 1916 [1]—that he was an earl. Then in 1783, Joshua Currey, a Loyalist lawyer of the third generation of colonial Curreys, removed from Peekskill to Gagetown, New Brunswick, where he established a race now widely scattered over the St. John River counties. Marin's maternal grandfather, the first Richard Currey, came up to New York from New Brunswick, about 1840, to make his way in the States, and married a girl of English descent, Eliza Gardner, of Union Hill, in New Jersey. Marin has liked to say that his ancestors were "of the best English Ale, Dutch Bitters, Irish Gin, French Vermouth and plain Scotch." [2] It is an amusing idea, and has been widely repeated, but the Marin cellar demonstrably houses only the vermouth and ale, with perhaps a dash of old Spanish sherry.

Marin's father was vaguely around to watch his son growing up: he ran for election to the Rutherford Township Committee in 1872, along with one John V. S. van Winkle, a descendant of the town's first well-to-do merchant. But as the years followed, his commissions as a public accountant, together with private investments in out-of-town business, kept him largely away. It was thirty-six years, as a matter of fact, before they ever slept under one roof—in a hotel in Venice. Marin, meanwhile growing up with his mother's relations, lived in an atmosphere—a point to be labored—as thoroughly Yankee as apple pie and baked beans. He even looked like aunts Jenny and Lelia and Uncle Dick Currey, who were all tall and thin, their

---

[1] The town of Union, situated on high ground above Weehawken, was consolidated with West Hoboken in 1925 to form Union City.

[2] *Letters of John Marin*, edited by Herbert J. Seligmann (New York, 1931), unpaged, letter to Egmont Arens, Stonington, Maine, August 26, 1928, near the end of the volume.

peaked faces distinguished by thin noses and the kind of pale, transparent skin that shows wrinkles early. He stopped growing when he reached five foot eight, somewhat short for male Curreys; but his bangs and his curls, which his wife, years later, trimmed under a saucepan, were a Currey nut brown, and not black like the straight hair of the Marins.

Grandfather Currey bought a peach farm in Delaware, three miles south of Milford, in the middle seventies, and for a few years the family traveled back and forth between Jersey village and Delaware orchard. Some of Eliza Currey's Gardner cousins had moved down from Union Hill to the Delaware country, and liking the life there, in the Mispillion Valley, had urged her to join them. When the Curreys followed, proceeding by sailboat and steamer from Jersey City to Wilmington, the journey gave Marin his first view of the ocean he was destined to paint.

It was on the Delaware farm, at the age of seven or eight, that Marin began to make pencil sketches. When Uncle Dick Currey, a Union Army sharpshooter at the age of eighteen, now hunted the orchards and woods with shotgun and retrievers, his nephew tagged after with pencil and paper. After seventy years, the artist remembers trying to show how conies bounded over the bracken; so that many years later, when he had learned to use color, he was predisposed to paint life in motion. Trees, birds, and ships; clouds, islands, and ocean: all these have lived and moved freely in the forty-year cycle of the mature Marin paintings.

After the close of the peach-orchard idyll, when he was kept indoors only briefly to read a daily chapter of Scripture and to do a few sums, Marin spent the winters, from ten to eighteen, in schools in New Jersey: public school, private academy, the preparatory department of Stevens Institute of Technology, and a year at the Institute proper. There was never a day in those years, so he says, when he would not have preferred to be out of doors—walking, drawing, or fishing. There was never a lesson, outside of geometry, that he felt had stayed learned. Only the summer days could be salvaged by a boy whose only bent was for angling, shooting, and sketching: days spent on the Jersey coast, or on the New Brunswick steamer; or best of all, in the Catskills, or at White Lake, in Sullivan County, New York, where the schoolboy was free to follow his fanciful hero, Natty Bumppo, into the wilderness—a box of paints and a pencil shoved into his pocket alongside of the fishhook and birdshot, a pad of good paper tucked under his arm.

In 1886 in the Catskills, near Slide Mountain, he made neat sketches of meadows enclosed by rail fences; of cows grazing beside their own shadows; of particular trees and particular mountains. There was nothing

5

precocious, there was nothing pretentious; but the drawings were executed with professional care and signed "J. C. Marin." Next year, in his washes from White Lake, of which a few are extant, Marin—not without fore-thought and planning—used the technique of saturating the whole paper with water. He had seen reproductions of water colors from England, he cannot say whose: perhaps plates of pictures by Turner, who "played with tonalities," as Marin describes him, and cared little for showing the solid, natural forms which may be existent under color and light. Or the young painter may have observed, in the books, how Peter de Wint and David Cox preserved the fresh bloom of their transparent colors through the use of wet paper. At any rate, he discovered that a brush full of color laid on moist paper will produce those poetic—if somewhat misty—effects. He also saw, early, how glimpses of unpainted white paper between the strokes of the brush make the colors glow and sparkle by contrast.

Yet the aquarelles made by Marin in his seventeenth year, for all they are sensitive, proved little more than a nice taste for color and a feeling for light: though one of them seems to anticipate the impressionist method which their author momentarily adopted exactly twenty years later in Paris. In one of the landscapes, the lake is represented by small patches of unblended color in various pastel hues.

After the school years, Marin tried to fit himself into his era's com-monplace, middle-class pattern. His father, remaining a comfortably well-off, self-possessed man, clearly expected him to earn a conventional living, while the aunts expounded the moral view of their day that a young man worth his salt ought to look for a job in the city. Marin obligingly went to work at Calhoun, Robbin's & Company's wholesale notion house, on lower Broadway, Manhattan, where he got into trouble by scrambling the orders which fell into his hands; and then, for nearly four years, he moved through a succession of architects' offices and painted on Sundays. Setting up his own office in 1893, he built six well-planned frame houses in Union Hill, including a residence—it is 523 Forty-eighth Street, Union City, today —for his aunts Jenny and Lelia. "My houses were plain, but they func-tioned for comfortable living," Marin has said of them. After that effort, he drifted around for three or four years, jotting down what he saw with pencil or paintbrush. The first pages of a sketchbook which survives from those years contain drawings influenced by the architectural studies: views of the Old State House in Philadelphia, for example, and old houses in Germantown. But by the time he got into Virginia, Marin was inventing his own private symbols for the American landscape.

There clearly had to be symbols in drawing, he seems to have thought,

6

because a sketch, at its best, only stands for nature's reality and can not duplicate it in substance or form. Nature and art, as he saw from the first, are unequal. Since no one had ever taken the trouble to tell him that draftsmen usually learned traditional symbols in art schools—symbols for trees, clouds, and the motion of rivers—Marin composed his own time-saving alphabet. Indeed, he began even then, on his own, to invent a new idiom, a new language, couched in the new form of writing. Most of the drawings made during a few months so far from home as St. Paul and Milwaukee, and on Lake Michigan and the Mississippi River, correspond, to be sure, to the nineteenth century's predilection for the scene's outward likeness; but the detail—of trees, say, and cloud forms—is contrived in an individual manner: for the artist, through a fortunate want of instruction, had been obliged to find his own means of expression. When he was older, he could say, looking backward, that he was early intent upon setting down the most frugal and definitive line. But it also happened that the line was already as personal as any man's handwriting is.

Some of the notebook titles for the individual drawings, one observes parenthetically, suggest Marin's characteristic choice of an abstract term for pointing out the quality of some particular scene. A poetic fragment of landscape, for instance, bears the name *Formation in Wisconsin*—a title which provides a small clue to the young artist's habit of looking for structure in nature. So it appears that subsequent years in Paris were hardly more than divertive. The passing interest he showed there in soft lights and tonalities and impressionist fancies merely postponed his systematic inquiries into the "formation" of nature.

In between journeys from home, Marin roamed his own countryside afoot and on bicycle. He knew by heart and by eye the Palisades of New Jersey, the meadows and ridges between the Hackensack and Passaic rivers —and drove his aunts to distraction with his unsettled habits. How would you have handled a young man in his twenties who traipsed all day through the woods and fiddled at night with clipped drawings from *Harper's New Monthly Magazine?* If you had given the boy the thirty dollars he wanted, what would he have bought? A good winter suit? Not at all! He would have got a set of that new Abbey Shakespeare. Don't you remember? He was crazy for Edwin A. Abbey through the middle nineties.

Of the scores of water colors which the artist remembers producing during the decade from 1888 to 1898, fewer than twenty remain. The earliest, from about 1891, have to do with houses and farms in the Weehawken region. They show some preoccupation with a painter's professional problems—perhaps beyond their author's self-tutored range at that

7

time—and always a lively and affectionate interest in the worn subject matter. The latest, and also the most "realistic," were painted in the state of Virginia in 1893: and herein lies a thesis. The newer the subject matter is to the painter, the less devious is his method of handling it. With Marin, familiarity breeds complication.

The painter was in his twenty-eighth year when the aunts admitted that since he was a failure at everything else, he might as well go to art school. (Their brother, Dick Currey, was no longer at hand to advise them one way or another. Married to Antoinette Pavée of Paris, and father of two little daughters, Lyda and Retta, he had died in 1895, to the lasting grief of his admiring nephew.) Marin's father, lately married to Mrs. Isabel (Wilson) Bittinger, mother of Charles Bittinger, the U. S. Navy painter and portraitist, agreed to keep John in funds at the Pennsylvania Academy of Fine Arts in Philadelphia, though he had some misgivings. Marin found the greater part of the academy students to be wealthy young women intent upon adding sketching to fancywork in their list of accomplishments. He was therefore not disposed to be greatly impressed by the tone of the place; he was so much in earnest. William Merritt Chase, the German-trained portraitist, was an able master of drawing from life, but students were expected to spend so much time on "pink antique" from old castings, and dissecting dead tramps under Thomas P. Anshutz, that Marin, in his two years of study, worked only once, in his regular classes, from a professional model.

He won, it was true, a prize for his drawings, though not for the drawings made from classical casts alongside of such colleagues as Arthur Beecher Carles, who became his close friend in Paris, and Joseph Hergesheimer, whose pictorial talent was later put to apt use in his novels. Marin won the prize for his Weehawken sketches of wild fowl and river boats drawn from close observation. The models for the only extant drawings from his academy days were students who posed for each other at unscheduled noonday meetings. Like a slightly later study of Miss Lelia Currey at the piano at which she taught for a living (Plate 1), these sketches, free in style and rich in tonality, show the author preoccupied with the total "formation" at an actual moment: somewhat in the manner of Constantin Guys, whose work Marin had not yet seen or heard of. Of the two student camps of the era, the one of Whistler, the other of Sargent, Marin took his place in the former. It is easy to see that the young man and his teachers—of whom Sargent, perhaps after Ingres, was the idol—could have drawn little comfort from their mutual contact.

"There was a boy in my class," Marin says, "who could transfer a Greek torso to paper and make it look nice and real—as real as the plaster

8

A. Headed for Boston, 1923 (water color)

cast that he copied. But I thought to myself, What's it for? A man paints a boat so it looks like a boat. But what has he got? The boat doesn't *do* anything. It doesn't move in the water, it is blown by no tempest. That copy-boat might sell boats, but it cannot be art. Art must show what goes on in the world." This is the moment animating the form.

Marin hung around the Philadelphia wharves when he got tired of copying inanimate figures and went home the next year to begin another six years of loafing. "I was a kid until I was thirty," he says. And if an objective pattern of work is a sign of maturity, it is true that he was still a boy at the turn of the century. Then he began to grow up. In some 5½" x 9" and 7" x 10" sketches, made up and down the near-by Dallytown Road, in Meek's Woods, the Hackensack Meadows, and along the North River, from 1900 to 1905, he paid close attention to technical matters such as the problem of light and the organization of masses. Association with artists and students had not been sheer waste, after all. He had been introduced to a wider view of the professional problems of artists, if not to the means by which he would solve them. Nothing could keep him now from working out the sober career to which nature had called him.

There are also preserved from the winters of 1903 and 1904 exactly one hundred 9" x 12" canvas panels whose color is still fresh and delightful. Using as medium a mixture of turpentine, linseed oil, and varnish, Marin worked out of doors, applying the pigments with the greatest rapidity, sometimes with palette knife, in midwinter temperatures which froze the paint to the canvas. Crowded with color and form, the little pictures explored the North River: the Palisades and the banks, the wide stream with its currents and endless movement of boats, and on the far side, the vertical life of Manhattan. Marin thinks of this work as largely intuitive, not so well schooled as the drawings. He received personal visions which he set down in color as directly as possible—and with a swiftness inspired by intemperate weather. One may see, in those one hundred small paintings, the Marin style and the Marin method in accidental process of making.

"I was looking at the world and wanted to put it down in paint, *all* of it," Marin has told me. Not yet possessed of the selective judgment which distinguishes his more mature work, he was yet enabled by his instinctive good taste to work a kind of order from the myriad forms which flashed through his visions, so that now and again there are glimpses of maturer effects. There is, for example, a simple composition in blue surrounded by bands of dark color, his first "frame within frame"; while the sky in another is laid down inside an abstract figure in black, as later, with more deliberate purpose, a patch of cloud or a ship would be nailed down in a rough square or rectangle, at once to accent relative compositional values and preserve equilibrium. These patterns must have proceeded quite urgently out of his head; he had seen nothing like them.

It is touching to think of that slight, boylike man, his wistful face frosted under a rimed circlet of bangs, his numbed fingers clutching his small, frozen paintings, trudging back from his work, at the close of the day, to the house in Weehawken where the two maiden aunts would regard his best efforts with sniffles. Not expecting, as many young painters are wont to do now, to sell his first fruits in a clamorous market, he tacked his unsigned and undated impressions to the walls of his top-story room; and there, with no word of encouragement, he spent hours alone with his quick, brightly colored renditions of nature. And as he sat in his chilly attic, wishing for a small word of praise or some exchange of ideas, the aunts would be thinking, "John ought to *do* something!" At least, that is what they would *say* when he came down for supper.

During the summer between those two crowded winters of painting, Marin spent a month on Cape Ann, in a borrowed packing-house studio in the old New England fishing center of Gloucester. Only one drawing —it hangs today in Charles Bittinger's Duxbury residence—is known to survive from that month in the picturesque harbor: a small colored-pencil and pastel sketch of the fishing sheds, the indications of architectural structure flushed with Turneresque atmosphere. The disappearance, attributable to a Weehawken charwoman during Marin's absence in Paris, of a group of washes which Marin remembers having painted at Gloucester, creates an unfortunate void in the artist's story. Five or six years later, he was making a respectable bid for acknowledgment in a field which had, after Winslow Homer, few weighty practitioners. The Gloucester drawings in the transparent medium might have helped to explain how, when he resumed it abroad in 1908, he was able to handle it with such virtuosity.

To please aunts Jenny and Lelia, who still felt that schools, while inferior to offices, were better than idleness, Marin spent a few weeks in the fall at the Art Students' League in Manhattan. But the lessons there never seemed of much use. If any teacher had tried to explain the complicated mechanics of color, as John Sloan has since done there so ably, Marin would not have listened. He already had his own pragmatic practice of color. He wished, to be sure, to give satisfaction with a competitive painting on the subject of Christ on the Mount, in which, in an effort to concentrate movement and light on the central figure, he left the faces of forms in the crowd quite unfinished. Hence his work was not liked. (If he had followed the example of Delacroix, who "finished" a fabulously

10

beautiful sketch to produce a rather tedious painting, in *Mirabeau and the Marquis de Dreux-Brézé,* would he not still, like the great French romantic, have failed to gain assent by the compromise?)

The trouble, of course, was not that Marin could not work realistically. He had occupied himself, at the age of sixteen, in working up drawings from engravings in *Harper's Young People.* He had copied the head of a horse after Rosa Bonheur, not omitting the marks of the point on the plate. But the engraver's methods were not Marin's methods. Academy fare was not Marin's dish. It was not long before he risked the auntly displeasure and went gratefully back to his own self-taught way.

The Inevitable Visit to Europe

Summer, 1905 — Spring, 1910

JOHN C. MARIN AGREED IN 1905 TO SEND HIS UNACCOUNT-able son over to Europe on Miss Currey's demand. "If John isn't going to do any work," said Aunt Jenny, "why, then, he might as well go to Paris with the rest of the idlers . . . . Especially," she sniffed, "since his step-brother Charles is over there, having his fling."

As a matter of fact, it was stepbrother Charles Bittinger who had proposed to his mother, now Mrs. John C. Marin, that young John ought to finish his studies in Europe. Mrs. Marin passed the suggestion on to her husband; and the senior Marin, though he thought John ought to *work,* like the next man, consulted Aunt Jenny. The women, between them, cajoled him against his better practical judgment: "So my father forked up once again," Marin says, "and I hit Paris in my thirty-fifth year."

In the early summer of 1905, he said goodbye to his family—and to his sweetheart, Miss Marie Jane Hughes, the reserved older sister of Miss Sarah Hughes, a lively and sociable seamstress who had sometime been employed by the maiden Curreys. Marie Jane had lately come down for a visit to Union Hill from the village of Coeymans, in the southeastern tip of Albany County, where her brothers worked the home farm bequeathed by their father, a Scotch-Irish immigrant from Protestant Ireland. Like Sarah, whose liveliness had somewhat dismayed the shy painter, Marie had dark hair, olive skin, and a small, rounded figure; but unlike her sister, who liked to play little jokes on the men, she was respectfully self-effacing at parties. There was an undefined understanding that Marie and the painter, who had never been lucky with the new sort of woman, somehow suited each other; and that if she waited, he might—who could tell?—come back one day from Europe and take her to wife. (Their next meeting occurred three years later, when the old understanding was not so much renewed as protracted.)

One of Marin's friends, reviving impressions stored up thirty years in his memory, describes how the artist looked when he made his first appearance in Bohemian Paris: "His lean, dry, somewhat swarthy face with its sharp nose already was reminding people of a wizened apple or the visage of a wren. A slight, medium-tall, somewhat slouchy figure, he had, together with the look of a Yankee farmer, the curious personal dignity and simplicity of the type. At excited moments, he also resembled his future water colors. His black *(sic)* hair would appear to be flying in a wedge from his head, and beneath it there would lie a brownish patch that was his face, and beneath that, a white band that was his collar, and basing it, an area of ultramarine that was his four-in-hand." [1] This was before the days of his new French mustache.

Charles Bittinger, experienced now in the ways of Bohemia, helped his Yankee stepbrother in the search for an attic room overlooking some possibly peaceful courtyard. They settled on 3 Rue Campagne Première, not above two city blocks from the Luxembourg. Looking not unlike the court in the etching, *Cour Dragon, Paris,* 1906 (Plate 2), it was also, since it was constantly filled with vendors and wandering minstrels, as unquiet as any left-bank courtyard in Paris. Charles introduced Marin to his art-loving bride, Edith Gay Bittinger, who had come to Paris from Radcliffe College to study for opera. Mrs. Bittinger took a great liking to this rather impersonal kinsman. "He was always so sweet when we all traveled together," she told me. The Bittingers made him acquainted with other American artists who frequented the sidewalk café called the Dôme, not far from the studio, and supervised the purchase of etching equipment with which the new arrival might eke out his allowance from home.

Marin had bought in New York, with the proceeds of his first sale of sketches—a batch of thirty at a dollar apiece—a translation of the *Traité de la gravure à l'eau-forte* by Maxime Lalanne, a widely admired landscape engraver of the eighteen seventies. The English version of the second French edition, made in 1880 by S. R. Koehler of Roxbury, Massachusetts, contained the editor's introductory chapter on the technical elements of the etcher's art, with specific directions for getting the best results the most cheaply. Koehler's bibliography introduced Marin to the several volumes of *L'Oeuvre complet de Rembrandt,* by Charles Blanc, and so to the finest view of the Dutch artist's etchings that a student could find in an American library. Ready now to try his hand at some plates of his own, he began to experiment with some of the techniques of etching. With the help of Koehler's manual and his practiced stepbrother, he learned how to dab the ground with white virgin wax, Burgundy pitch, and Egyptian asphaltum; to smoke and varnish and incise the fixed ground with a point; to bathe the plate in a mordant; and to pull his own prints.

After a few aimless sittings in the drawing classes of various well-known

[1] Paul Rosenfeld, "John Marin's Career," *New Republic* (April 14, 1937), p. 289.

teachers, self-imposed repetitions of his attendance upon art schools at home, Marin set out by himself to explore the byways of Paris, in emulation of a newly discovered Parisian engraver. The son of an otherwise irreproachable London physician and a French dancing girl with whom the doctor enjoyed an "unlicensed connexion," Charles Méryon had invented a new style of etching, with broadened handling and simplified means.[2] Méryon's techniques were said to be slow and laborious, like fastidious writing, but his effects looked direct and poetic. A favorite of Charles Baudelaire, whose opinion was weighty, Méryon was *par excellence* the portrayer of Paris. Marin, vastly admiring *La Morgue* (1850), a riverside view of Browning's "Doric little Morgue" on the Seine, set out to follow in Méryon's footsteps. No other guide could have suited him better.

The etchings of 1905 were not printed for sale. Some of the prints were thought by their author to lack professional realization, and the dealers were cool to those the artist thought finished. They preferred the tight finish of Lalanne to the loose treatment of Méryon. The trial proofs that remain do not invariably show a borrowed approach to the medium; they do not all resemble Méryon's atmospheric impressions. Indeed, in the best of them, sharp, bold lines enclose subject matter in a kind of geometrical movement such as came to characterize so much of the painting. The overtones are poetic, as in the French etcher's prints, but the rhythms march more quickly than Méryon's.[3]

The fugitive *Noons* and *Nocturnes* of J. A. M. Whistler, who had died only two years earlier, were high fashion in the more advanced circles in Paris in 1905. Hence the dealers were wont to say to the novices, "Now if you would do something like Whistler—if you *won't* make realistic Lalannes—we could probably sell it." They dwelt on the wistful line, the soft atmosphere, that new collectors looked for in etchings. So Marin did produce a French Whistler of sorts by wiping the plates in J. A. M.'s manner to increase the intrinsic range of tonalities; but ironically finding no market, he concluded that Rembrandt was really more in his style: although, oddly enough, the notebooks at home showed that Marin with pencil was closer to Whistler than to Rembrandt van Rijn in the matter of line. The trouble was simply that with a point in his hand, Marin wanted to do things that pertained to the point and not to the pencil. Early in 1906, he paid a memorial visit to Amsterdam, whither Rembrandt had gone at the age of twenty. Only two or three of the Amsterdam etchings seemed, after so

---

[2] *See* (Sir) Frederick Wedmore, *Méryon and Méryon's Paris* (London, 1892).

[3] *John Marin*, Museum of Modern Art (New York, 1936). Nos. 1 to 8 in the check-list of etchings compiled by E. M. Benson.

much pains, to be worth the printing.[4] The others all turned out under-bitten.

Meanwhile, just before Christmas that first year in Paris, aunts Jenny and Lelia Currey sent their nephew a five dollar bill as a present, advising him, in the cliché of the period, to smoke it. Marin, lighting his pipe for a fact—although not with the bill—set fire to a panel of burlap which a former tenant had hung on the sloping walls of the studio. The police and the firemen arrived simultaneously and quarreled over the matter of jurisdiction and credit while the flames and the smoke spoiled most of the artist's meager possessions.

On the way to Amsterdam, sometime after Christmas, Marin made a side trip to Knocke-sur-Mer, a watering place twenty miles east of Ostend, in West Flanders. On the road to his inn from the station, he ran into the Bittingers, whom he had expected to meet later at Bruges, on the main line to Holland, and in the excitement he handed to a porter, who dropped it, a handbag containing a bottle of perchloride of iron, intended for use as a mordant in etching. The spilled acid destroyed all the clothes which remained after the fire. Marin was undismayed. Possessions, he has always maintained, are a bother. Mrs. Bittinger observed the next day, when John, full of plans for new work, seemed unready to go on to Ostend in spite of need for replacements, that a fixed if somewhat negative theorem governed his travels: he was never willing to leave *any* place that he happened to visit. His movements today reflect such postponements. He likes to work wherever he is at the moment.

Seven plates were etched in 1906 at Laon, the ancient Roman hill town of Laudunum, eighty-seven miles northeast of Paris. One of these plates, a near view of the twelfth-century cathedral, was printed in an edition of forty. All of Laon's famous towers appeared in one plate or another. Twenty-two additional plates were etched in the remaining months of that year, all but five made in Paris and nearly half of them published in editions of from six to about fifty prints. From here on, the artist signed himself simply "Marin."

The best of the 1906 plates from the provinces, *Moulin St. Maurice, Marne River*, was made in Meaux, a cathedral city since the fourth century, on the right bank of the Marne some thirty miles northeast of Paris. Thirty prints were struck off. An unremarkable oil painting which he made there, *The Mills of Meaux*, was sold to the French government in a transaction engineered by George Oberteuffer, an American impressionist

---

[4] Nos. 9 and 10 in the Benson check-list. A good print of *Bridge at Amsterdam*, 15⅞" x 7½", may be seen in the collection of the Art Institute of Chicago.

painter who played billiards with Marin in Paris. Oberteuffer, it appears, introduced the Minister of Fine Arts to Marin and jockied him into buying the painting for 400 francs. Other views of Meaux having failed to come off, Marin returned the next year to etch the medieval Cathedral of St. Stephen. Well-made prints of that etching were tipped into copies of the *Gazette des Beaux-Arts,* with a comment to the effect that while M. Marin's water colors and engravings were a little frail as to structure *(squelette),* they were seductively Whistleresque in their sensibility.[5]

In 1907, more or less by design, Marin went to meet his father, step-mother, and Edith and Charles Bittinger in glamorous Venice. The artist, wandering about unannounced, came upon them one day in the plaza. Marin *père,* already vexed by a published cartoon by Marius de Zayas, the Mexican caricaturist, showing young John playing poker with some of his friends at the American Club, inquired now, at a table at Florian's, what his son, nearly forty, had to show for the father's investment. A hand-ful of etchings, mostly unsalable . . . a painting somewhere in a provincial museum. Marin tried to explain that he played billiards, not poker, with people like Will Simmons, a highly refined young engraver of monkeys and eagles, and Lionel Walden, a Luxembourg medalist, and George Ober-teuffer, who knew French officials. He listened respectfully while Mrs. Marin, who believed in his future, coaxed him to make a few etchings that the public would like—though he refused her invitation to mount the Grand Canal in a gondola, to the *Accademia,* to visit an exhibition of Whistler's etchings in a gallery accustomed to Tintorettos and Titians. He didn't want to imitate Whistler, he told her. (Back in New York, it turned out, the Marins called on Louis Katz, the print dealer, who promised to call at John's studio on his next visit to Paris; and the Katz connection, with Mrs. Marin as a paying client, helped to smooth Marin's way in Europe for the next two or three years.)

Twenty plates were etched in Venice that season. Marin drew the pic-turesque churches: St. Mark's on the plaza, Santa Maria della Salute, the clock tower of Santa Maria Zobenigo, the campanile of San Pietro's and San Rocco's; a number of the more remarkable bridges: Paradiso, Ghetto, San Pantaleo, Donna Onesta; and the usual canal and street scenes. Henry McBride, a painter and teacher before he went to the New York *Sun* as art critic, five years later, subsequently reported that he had seen the artist in Venice, where he seemed to be "incorrigibly immersed in the business of interrogating nature." He also noted that Marin had, even then, the

---

[5] November, 1908, p. 398.

"hatchet-hewn face" which Gaston Lachaise memorialized in a bronze portrait twenty years afterwards.[6]

When Mrs. Charles Bittinger came down with typhoid fever in Venice, the family sent for her sister to come with a nurse from Johns Hopkins hospital. The fever having conveniently broken by the time Miss Mary Gay and the nurse arrived from the States, the Marins formed boating parties that sound, in Mrs. Bittinger's telling, like the stately diversions in the Henry James novels of Venice. Marin, impartially courting the American ladies—Miss Gay with prints of his etchings, and the nurse with excursions to the glassworks at Murano—decided to remove his Parisian mustache. The barber called in the police to report that a probable criminal was attempting to arrange a disguise. This episode is said by his friends to account for a lifelong aversion to barbers.

Back in Paris after brief visits to Rome and Florence, Marin was surprised to discover, for the first time in his life, that he had something to sell. He had made no conscious effort, he thought, to compromise with the market, but the etchings were charming. Louis Katz liked what he saw on his next trip to Paris and offered a market for which Marin pulled from twenty-five to thirty prints from each of eighteen plates etched in Venice. In the following season, Katz sold $2,000 worth of the etchings. The published plates of the year 1907 totaled twenty-seven, the Venetian portfolio augmented by street scenes from Paris (Plate 3). Five Venetian prints and three earlier pieces (Paris, Meaux, Laon) were reproduced in *L'Art Décoratif* for January, 1908, with a friendly critique by Charles Saunier, who described Marin's line as rapid, nervous, passionate, and elegant, and spoke of the artist's insistence on "function" as against the prevailing French fashion for impressionist tones. With the same issue of the French periodical, the subscribers received a handsomely printed original etching, *Through the Window, Venice*, which the editors had bought up from the artist.

In 1908, Marin further gratified his stepmother and his dealer on Avenue Weber by etching three landmarks of Paris—Notre Dame, L'Opéra, and the Madeleine—in more conventional style: beautifully realized and with ample detail to aid recognition; but, compared to the free style he was using in Venice, frankly commonplace in achievement. There was also a large realistic etching of St. Sulpice, of which two states were printed but not offered for sale. There were no other plates from that year for two reasons: Marin was much on the wing, out in the country, back to the States on a visit, and over the Channel to England; and he resumed work

---

[6] *John Marin*, Museum of Modern Art Catalogue, p. 11.

at that time with the transparent colors that have since made him famous.

Critical comment on the etchings has sometimes been impaired by the want of exact chronological knowledge of the artist's development. In the Alfred Stieglitz memorial exhibition at the Museum of Modern Art in New York in the summer of 1947, for example, there was an installation of prints which was intended to be a witty revelation of Marin's artistic history. A print of *L'Opéra,* the 1908 potboiler, was followed by De Zayas' sharp caricature of Marin and Stieglitz.[7] Then came a print of Cézanne's small *Bathers,* and some later Manhattan etchings by Marin. Edward Alden Jewell, translating the visual story as it was intended, reported the sequence as follows: "Marin, not yet introduced to modernism, meets Stieglitz, who shows him a Cézanne, with the result typified by the striking change in Marin's style."[8] The little joke loses its point in the light of any one of a number of etchings, such as a 1907 Paris street scene in which rooks take flight over a ruinous tower. It is pure Marin, the Marin of the theoretical etchings of Lower Manhattan; yet it was made two years before the artist's meeting with Stieglitz.

Marin has kept a few water colors made on his excursion to Meaux in 1907, representational sketches of mills raised on piles in the river, and a small sheaf of wash drawings which, according to his best recollection, were made in mid-ocean, on the return voyage to Europe after a three months' visit at home in 1908. These pictures, atmospheric impressions of shipboard and ocean in broad planes of color, look backward, not forward. But in France, in the autumn of 1908, he began, in some of the pictures, to build the color blocks into structures. There is a street scene of that year in which the houses are assembled from patches of gray tones and violet, built block above block, as a mason would lay a sound wall. Charles Bittinger, who bought the water color at Stieglitz's gallery in 1911, said he had observed, at the time it was made, that a new and individual style had made its appearance in Paris. If in its delicate harmonies it reminded people of Whistler, it was at once stronger and warmer, as Paul Rosenfeld thought, than the latter's wash drawings.[9] Several water colors of 1908 and 1909 illustrate the new vigor and fresh use of color.

While these washes were new in the Marin cycle, two of their newest ideas were not strange in post-impressionist circles. Cézanne, who had taken his rightful place as a master as lately as 1904,[10] with a retrospective show

[7] Reproduced in *Camera Work,* No. XLVI (April, 1914).

[8] The New York *Times* (June 15, 1947), p. 10X.

[9] "John Marin's Career," *New Republic* (April 14, 1937), pp. 289-292.

[10] He had been under serious discussion even among the generality of painters only since 1895, the year Ambroise Vollard gave him his first representative exhibition.

at the Autumn Salon, had demonstrated, by word and by deed, the pictorial value of structure versus tonality; [11] while Georges Seurat, the hero of many young modernists of the School of Paris, had preached the doctrine of "divisionist" colors.

Seurat, having dug into the color researches of Michel Eugène Chevreul—whose work, *De la loi du contraste simultané des couleurs* (1839), had grown out of experimentation at the Gobelins factories—had come up with a scientific notion of color with which he attempted to correct the "disorder" of impressionist workmanship. The "scientific impressionists," as they were called by Pissarro, studied and used the pointillist techniques evolved by Seurat, including the use of "divided" (i.e., unmixed) color from Chevreul's list of four hues and their intermediate tones: blue and the tones of blue leading to red; red and the red tones leading through orange to yellow; yellow and the yellow tones verging on green; and green with the tones completing the circle to blue.

Now I do not discover that Marin ever went in deliberately for such highly technical studies. The evidence seems to show that he was no "scientific impressionist" such as described by Pissarro. Moreover, his stepbrother and sister, as well as Marin himself, retain the impression that he was unfamiliar with the work of Cézanne before 1911. Yet of such and such, of Cézanne and Seurat, was the talk of the painters whom he saw at the Dôme; such was the professional *ambiance* that he touched on in Paris. He could not have escaped it: and certainly something very like the first three segments of Chevreul's circle of colors came in time to dominate Marin's palette, while something like Cézanne's passion for structure has made the younger man's style rugged and durable.[12]

A water color notably illustrating the evolution of Marin's personal style was made at the end of December, 1908, when the artist crossed the English Channel from Havre to place some prints with a dealer in London. He was there only three days, in the midst of a snowstorm, but he made a painting that came out in the way, as he said, that he thought he would like it (Plate 4). In trying to put down an omnibus to show what it did and how he himself felt about it, he "played around" [13] with patches of color instead of projecting the object with lines. The picture—it became

---

[11] *Paul Cézanne: Letters,* edited by John Rewald (London, 1941), letter CLXXIV to Charles Camoin, p. 241; cf. the letters to Émile Bernard in the same volume.

[12] More discussion of the apparent "look" of Cézanne in one phase of Marin will necessarily follow.

[13] A term constantly used in Marin's talk about painting, "playing around" is illustrated, when he speaks, with sculptural, ambidextrous gestures that show what is meant. The reader must imagine extremely articulate fingers playing a Bach fugue in the air.

the first item in the Stieglitz collection of upwards of two hundred Marins —proved to be better than he could normally do at the time (Plate 5), for in only a few of the French water colors of the following year, as in *Four O'Clock on the Seine* (Plate 6), did he use the pictorial shorthand which was in process of invention for the purpose of animating restrained patterns of color. *Four O'Clock on the Seine* was simple in the sum of its parts, but a new way of looking into nature was there, together with answers to some of the "interrogations"; and the new way of putting everything rapidly down is distinctly suggested.

In a letter to the biographer (June 19, 1947), Marin said, apropos painting that picture, "I was confronted with a gray bank of clouds—in the desire to break through I slapped in strong round spots of blue—then I was satisfied that I had broken through with the effect obtained." It is plain that his interrogations were already leading him beyond the momentary appearance of nature. And in revolting from the conventional way of putting down surface appearance, it was his intention, he says, not to put things down obviously. He preferred to let the spectator "look around a little."

While Marin's style was thus forming in Paris, an instrument was being prepared in New York for its effective introduction to possible patrons. In 1905, the year Marin crossed over to Europe, Edward Steichen—he spelled his name "Edouard" in those days—and his friend Alfred Stieglitz, exponents of art in photography, began to receive their disciples in the attic rooms of a brownstone house on Fifth Avenue, at No. 291, between Thirtieth and Thirty-first streets, close to the old Holland House where Bohemia went for its lunch when it had any money. Members of the coterie surrounding Stieglitz and Steichen, having withdrawn from the Camera Club at 3 West Twenty-eighth Street, called themselves Photo-Secessionists and required a gallery. They already had an eloquent mouthpiece, a quarterly journal called *Camera Work,* which appeared in January, 1903, with Alfred Stieglitz, theretofore publisher of *Camera Notes* for the Camera Club, as chief editor. Among their propagandists were such men of letters as Charles H. Caffin, Benjamin de Casseres, Sadakichi Hartmann, the flamboyant "King of Greenwich Village," and Paul Haviland, of the French family of porcelain manufacturers. Three small fourth-floor rooms at No. 291, furbished up by the Steichens, now (1905) became the show window for the new "art"—or for "the smeary compound of mush and mezzo tint which they have christened the 'new photography,'" as James Huneker put it. The newspapers reported that visiting ladies wore pants when they went to look at the photographs of Annie W. Brigman and Baron de Meyer.[14]

Then sometime in 1907, Steichen had, it is said, made this suggestion to Stieglitz: "Along with our art-in-photography photographs, why not show the anti-photographic in art?" The partners were pleased by this piquant idea and forthwith, in January, 1908, they showed fifty-eight water-color drawings by Auguste Rodin in the first public exhibition of that French sculptor's work in America. When Henri Matisse was given his first American showing the following April, some of the members, debating such issues as "Is Matisse a charlatan?" further seceded from the Photo-Secessionists on the ground that the galleries were being devoted to the baser arts of drawing and painting. This was the year, it should be remembered, when that brave group, The Eight—Henri, Sloan, Glackens, Lawson, Maurice Prendergast, Luks, Shinn, and Davies—dared to show serious paintings of Negroes and wrestlers, of hairdressers and pitchmen, of pickpockets and spielers, and were called "ash-can" artists by respectable people.

A second and more ominous crisis arose later that year in the affairs of the remnant of Photo-Secessionists. The rent for their three cozy rooms was advanced beyond the amount that Stieglitz and Steichen could conveniently raise and a lugubrious seamstress was thrust into the chambers. The adaptable Steichens, Edward and Clara, transformed an "unspeakable garrett" across the dark hallway and the so-called "Little Galleries" were born. A cheerful opening on the night of the first of December, after a dinner for members at Mouquin's, disclosed that the "Galleries" consisted of one unheated fifteen-foot room for the exhibition of pictures and a tiny office with a potbellied stove as a hangout for Stieglitz and the Saturday visitors. In the center of the small picture room stood a square wooden platform disguised with green burlap; and on this boxlike object, which might have served as a bench in the unfurnished gallery, there reposed a brass bowl from whose depths Marsden Hartley, the witty new painter from Maine, said he expected to see the wraith of James A. McNeill Whistler ascend over the company.

Caricatures of New York social and theatrical gentry by Marius de Zayas, the Mexican cartoonist on the New York *Evening World*, were shown at "291" the following January. Then Steichen, himself a theatrically handsome young man in that day, took a house with a garden in Giverny, the Norman town where Cézanne used to paint, and shipped home to Stieglitz from Paris a few water colors which an unknown John Marin had just shown at the American Club.

---

[14] For a more flattering description of the Photo-Secessionist gallery, see Jerome Mellquist in *The Emergence of an American Art* (New York, 1942), pp. 184 ff.

Although Marin had been diffident about showing himself to the great people of Europe, like Rodin and Matisse, and was wholly unknown to Leo and Gertrude Stein, the celebrity makers—"I was never one to push myself forward," he says—he had made the acquaintance of Steichen through Arthur B. Carles, his Philadelphia colleague, and Steichen had found the new water colors of street scenes and bridges in Paris about as anti-photographic as anything he had seen from American sources. Stieglitz hung them up at "291" in March, 1909, along with fifteen oil paintings by Alfred Maurer, a fellow expatriate.

Maurer, a former pupil of William M. Chase, had courageously abandoned an academic success in New York to become "modern" in Paris, where the Steins called him "Alfy." Having been taken up by the Steins, at whose celebrated salon at 27 rue de Fleurus he was asked to "explain" the works of Cézanne and Matisse to crowds of curious strangers, he was dismayed to find his new work very sharply received by satirical critics. Joseph Chamberlain wrote of one of his paintings: "What is it, a bursted tomato? a fireman's hat? a couple of people under an umbrella?"[15] Marin's pictures were looked upon somewhat more kindly. James Huneker, who generally took a favorable view of "291," described the exhibition as a duel in fire and shadow—Maurer supplying the fire and Marin the mist. He spoke of the poetic symbolism of Marin's "delicious tonalities," of his preoccupation with movement.[16] Although Marin's color harmonies came even then from the paint box, not from nature, they wore the look of conviction. But there was, on the whole, nothing in them, as Henry McBride recalled some years later, to disturb the "sensibilities of purists."[17]

Paul Haviland's summary in *Camera Work* of Marin's reception boasted that the new water colors were "pronounced by authorities" to be "the best examples of the medium which have ever been shown in New York."[18] The reviews, as Stieglitz himself had compiled them—and as elsewhere appearing in the press of the day—did not, as a matter of fact, add up to any such general impression. Outside of the circle of Stieglitz's friends, there was only Joseph Chamberlain to predict, at that time, that Marin would become a celebrity. And there was not, when you came down to it, actually much indication in the 1909 exhibition that Marin, the shy lyric poet, would one day blossom out as a natural dramatist. The papers were charming and fresh, but the stout framework and tough sinew of nature had not yet been re-

---

[15] New York *Evening Mail* (April 3, 1909), Editorial Section, p. 5.
[16] New York *Sun* (April 7, 1909).
[17] *John Marin*, Museum of Modern Art Catalogue, p. 12.
[18] July, 1909, pp. 27 f.

vealed. The artist had not yet wholly transferred his personal idiom from the copper plate to the paper. Yet there was something for Charles H. Caffin to go on when that critic, of the staff of the New York *Sun* and *International Studio,* wrote in a prophetic Note for the catalogue: "In some [of the water colors], the impression of locality and of enlivening figures is vivid; in most, however, the consciousness of facts disappears in a spiritualized vision of form and color."

Marin stayed on in Europe for a little more than a year after his first New York exhibition. He met Stieglitz during the summer in Paris; [19] he printed four etchings—the Cathedral at Chartres (Plate 7), two views of the Frauenkirche at Nuremberg, and a section of the Pflanzbadstrasse in Strasbourg—for Katz in New York and Albert Roullier of Chicago; and he was photographed in the artistic manner, his dark hair falling in prominent bangs over his slim, sensitive face. (Two American schoolgirls had tittered one night in a restaurant over "that Frenchman's wig," and Marin had pulled at his bangs, just to show them. . . .) And just before coming home, he visited Kufstein, on the east bank of Lower Inn Thal in the Austrian Tyrol. It was rumored in Paris that he had a girl with him; his friends hoped it was so. He was always so serious.

The low-keyed water colors (Plates 8, 9) which he painted at Kufstein, in the heart of the mountains, showed no advance in his style. But if he seemed more concerned with light and atmosphere than with movement and form, the explanation is simple. The terrain was new and there was not enough time, the way his eye and mind worked, to get under the surface. If he had been able to linger on for some months, he would doubtless have gone on from the surface "look" to the structure, as he had done, though incompletely, in Paris, and as he was to do so roundly in every new place, granting time, for the next forty years.

Reviewers who saw his first one-man show—forty-three water colors, twenty pastels, and eight etchings hung at "291" in February, 1910—compared the French aquarelles to music and poetry. William D. MacColl, writing in *Camera Work,* said that the artist's "certainties of color" had been fixed to the paper like beautiful words hammered into a lyric. Echoing words of Saint Paul, MacColl wrote, "To create lovely things one must see lovely things, hope lovely things, and desire lovely things, and that is what John Marin, in his intense and simple fashion, is greatly doing." [20] Israel L. White of the Newark *Evening News* quoted James Russell Lowell: "The art

---

19 See Jerome Mellquist, "John Marin: Painter from the Palisades," *Tricolor* (May, 1945), pp. 58-64, for a somewhat subjective account of the meeting.
20 April, 1910, pp. 41-44.

of effective writing," Lowell had written, "is to know how much to leave in the ink pot." So with good painting. And Marin had put down enough with no surfeit: for example, a bridge which was simple indeed in its elements, yet sufficiently solid to withstand a flood.[21]

Elizabeth Luther Cary, thinking perhaps of *London Omnibus,* now first shown, and of the few Seine River water colors that nearly resemble it, wrote in the New York *Times* on the subject of Marin's realization of structure through color.[22] Apparently the first of the critics to suggest that Marin owed a debt to Cézanne, Miss Cary stated a thesis which has become almost folkloric in the accepted picture of the artist at work. And it might have been shown, in all truth, that Cézanne and Marin had much in common. Both have approached their work from visible motifs; neither was ever bent on pure representation; both built up structures with color, although Marin's treatment of planes was not, in 1909–1910, so advanced as Cézanne's; and they shared a reclusive, mystical, undivided attachment to nature. Later on, three additional surface likenesses grew apparent: their regard for the superior values of the primary colors, though Cézanne, as we know, thought less of color than structure;[23] a dependence on pictorial symbols; and preoccupation with the manipulation of planes—an unequal preoccupation, it ought to be noticed, for in the purely lyrical paintings, which comprise more than half of Marin's output of approximately sixteen hundred pictures, there are few analytical traces. Yet individuality, the crowning aspect of style, received its due (if as yet quiet) expression, even in 1910, in the work of John Marin. If the hand was his own, so was the voice, though overtones of Cézanne could be heard by the listener.[24]

(Originality is not, in any case, one supposes in passing, the primary quality to search for in a new work of art. Originality, merely substituting strange context for creative thought, may produce an undistinguished limp watch in a conventional landscape; originality may provoke such a couplet as one of Herrick's to Julia:

> *Fain would I kiss my Julia's dainty leg,*
> *Which is as white and hairless as an egg.*

Hence it is not originality but individuality that trained taste first of all craves in a new work of creation—the acutely personal expression of a warmly felt observation, impression, idea, by a disciplined artist in possession of such private resources of hand, mind, and spirit as will make the

[21] Reprinted, *Camera Work* (April, 1910), p. 46.
[22] *Ibid.,* p. 45.
[23] *Paul Cézanne: Letters,* letter CLXXI to Emile Bernard, p. 239.
[24] See E. M. Benson, *John Marin, The Man and His Work* (Washington, 1935), pp. 16 ff., for a discussion of Marin as poet and Cézanne as scientist.

familiar seem new, or newly revealed, and fresh and delightful. . . .)

Some of the water colors in the 1910 exhibition bore such prophetic titles as *Hill and Village No. 1* and *Hill and Village No. 2,* by way of universalizing the particulars of two views of St. Rémy Chevreuse. Most of the "pastels" were impressions of Venice. About 12" x 14" in size, they were made on gray paper, some with colored pencils such as Marin had commonly used in the States, some with the crayons whose use he cultivated in Europe. He did not follow up the pastel techniques for the reason that the medium seemed to him to be fugitive. He found it difficult to get down to the definitive line with a crayon. It was better, he thought, to draw with lead pencil, even in washes.

"Around nineteen hundred and nine," wrote Marsden Hartley, many years later, "I met with a certain picture in water colour of a scene in Piccadilly, London—which was of course of a bus and all that gathers around it—and this water colour impressed me as different because it was not sweet and dainty, and later, on the outer edge of this rectangle, I saw a curious man who might have been a joker at the grave of Yorick. . . ." [25]

Hartley, whose own pictures had been hung at "291" for the first time in May, 1909, after the Marin-Maurer exhibition, might have seen *London Omnibus* in the 1910 exhibition, but it was not until some months later that he could have met the artist who reminded him of the gravedigger, that dry-witted descendant of Adam in *Hamlet.* As Hartley wandered around among the "grotesque-looking" people who visited Stieglitz in the small attic rooms, he bethought him not of Cézanne but of Whistler; yet he had to admit that Marin's pictures were not exactly "whistlerish." A strong new painter thus surveyed Marin's walls and saluted a colleague who had handled his medium in an individual way; neither after Whistler, nor, more surprisingly, after Winslow Homer, who was generally thought at the time to have said the first and last American word about water colors. [26]

Marin's debut spilled over into the following months, when a few of his pictures were hung in a show at "291"—from March 21 to April 15—along with the works of Arthur B. Carles, Arthur Dove, Marsden Hartley, Alfred Maurer, another new painter, Max Weber, and Steichen and others. Perhaps because the oil paintings which dominated the exhibition were bold and bright and exciting—and because Marin had been so lately under discussion—his French water colors were barely mentioned in the press reports of that showing. If he was unhappy about it, there was no time to show it. He was getting ready to leave Europe forever.

---

[25] "As to John Marin, and his ideas," *John Marin,* Museum of Modern Art Catalogue, p. 15.
[26] Winslow Homer had painted his last painting in November, 1909 (Lloyd Goodrich, *Winslow Homer* [New York, 1945], p. 199).

The American Landscape

Summer, 1910—1917

IN MAY, 1910, AFTER ARRANGING FOR THE HANGING OF TEN water colors in the *Salon d'Automne* of that year, Marin returned to the States on the Dutch steamer, *Nieuw Amsterdam*. Partly because New York had been livened up by a burst of new building and partly because it merely seemed fresh and lively after slow-moving Europe, Marin settled down to paint the racing streets and the quickening rivers. Paris, he had thought, was a quiet and beautiful woman in a dim gray room. New York was a man, swift and dynamic, striding along in the bright, sparkling air. Familiar with the North River from childhood, with the old wharves and vessels, he now caught the city's new motions—the horizontal stretch of the East River bridges, the flat sweep of gathering traffic on water and land, the vertical thrust of the tall Woolworth Building, which he bent in his paintings to meet the fast-moving Island. (It is said that Cass Gilbert, the architect, looked at Marin's version of his unfinished masterpiece at the Armory Show three years later and was overcome by a painful emotion.) [1]

A letter to Stieglitz, who had promised enough money to live on economically until pictures were sold, describes Marin's excitement in "piling New York's great houses one upon another with paint as they do pile themselves up there so beautiful, so fantastic." [2] Although there were times of depression, "little fits of the blues," while he struggled to give structure and form to his newest impressions, he was soon able to make it appear in his paintings that Manhattan Island was sentient. He spent the rest of the year on his metropolitan paintings, basing his forays on the Union Hill residence of the Misses Currey, his aunts. Then in 1911, the year of Cézanne's (and Picasso's) debut at Stieglitz's gallery, [3] and of the first American showing of his own Tyrolese pictures, he went with the aunts to the Berkshires, spending a month at Egremont Plains, a village set in the hills just north of Mount Everett and a few miles west of Mount Warner.

The landscapes made there were arrangements of color planes loosely

---

[1] Matthew Josephson, "Leprechaun on the Palisades," *New Yorker* (March 14, 1942), pp. 26-32.
[2] *Letters of John Marin*, undated letter to Stieglitz in Europe, first page of text.
[3] Alfred Stieglitz introduced Gertrude Stein to an American audience the following year by printing her comical pieces about Matisse and Picasso in a special Spring issue of *Camera Work*.

washed on, side by side, in broad sweeps. They illustrate the artist's growing concern for saving the flatness of paper while creating space and distance in color—not with line, as in drawing. Marin had just looked at Cézanne with a deliberate eye for the first time in his life, and his approach, there at Egremont, to the technical problem of laying on flat planes of color resembled that of the great man from Provence. Thus he made another important advance in the acquisition of the professional means of his era.

In the summer of 1912, he went up to the Adirondacks with Marie Jane Hughes, who, to observe the proprieties, invited another young woman to join them. They were engaged now, Marie Hughes and Marin, and talked of marriage during the following winter. Marie Jane went along on the painting trips daily, just as she was to do, almost daily, for the rest of her life.

The pictures the artist began at once to make in the mountains and swamps illustrate his undisturbed habit of "interrogating nature for himself," as McBride so well put it; of looking at new terrain at close range and, unlike Cézanne in the aquarelles, of setting down first of all what he saw. (Cézanne, on the contrary, rarely expressed the result of his first direct apprehensions. Retaining that first surface look in his head, instead of laying it down on the paper, he preferred, when he dipped brush into color, to go straight after the motif's theoretical aspect and to treat its internal structure architectonically.) But after refreshing his memory at the wellsprings of nature—a notable effect of which year-by-year habit is that there are no divisible, chronological "periods" into which his work falls—Marin did not then, as in most subsequent years, undertake the theoretical treatment of his well-studied motifs.

He had already begun on Manhattan, having the island now whole and by heart, to "do things" to the prevailing lines of the city, the horizontals and verticals: locking them up in circular motion, or, as with flintflake and rock, striking them sharply together to make the sparks fly. The water colors of the summer of 1912, as it happens, engaged in no such pyrotechnics. As in the Tyrol, and only once or twice afterwards, the final step was not taken. The pictures of swamps with dead trees represent merely the paschal revival which has always kept Marin from falling into the hackneyed manners that, in long spans of painting, have trapped all but the great. The pictures do not photograph swamps nor are they abstractions of "swamp." They simply look tangled and damp; they give off the idea and feeling of swamps in a personal idiom. When I came upon them one day in the studio—they were unsigned, undated—Marin said, with emotion, "Those are my swamps! I've always loved a good swamp!"

27

Believing, next winter, that he had got into his stride,[4] with the future secure to the artist, if only doubtfully to a man with a family, Marin married Miss Marie Jane Hughes, the kindly and birdlike young woman who had waited so long for him, biding her seven biblical years with such womanly acquiescence; and on their honeymoon to the national capital, after the marriage at Grove Church on December 7, the painter went on with his painting, producing a view of the mile-long Great Falls, some fifteen miles above Washington on the Potomac. The bride and groom came home in time for the *vernissage,* just after the first of the year, of Marin's annual exhibition at "291," the third since his return from Paris, and settled down for the winter and spring in the house of Sarah Hughes Shaw—Mrs. Marin's newly widowed sister, the fun-loving dressmaker—who lived now at 402 East Fifteenth Street in the Flatbush section of Brooklyn.

Before his marriage, Marin had composed, at Stieglitz's request, a brief catalogue Note to interpret the Manhattan pictures that were hung side by side, in the Little Galleries, with the Essex swamps and the Egremont hills:

> "*Shall we consider,*" he said, "*the life of a great city as confined simply to the people and animals on its streets and in its buildings? Are the buildings themselves dead? We have been told somewhere that a work of art is a thing alive. . . . Therefore if these buildings move me they too must have life. Thus the whole city is alive; the buildings, people, all are alive; and the more they move me the more I feel them to be alive.*
>
> "*It is this 'moving of me' that I try to express,*" he continues, "*so that I may recall the spell I have been under and behold the expression of the different emotions that have been called into being. How am I to express what I feel so that its expression will bring me back under the spell? Shall I copy facts photographically?*
>
> "*I see great forces at work; great movements; the large buildings and the small buildings; the warring of the great and the small; influences of one mass on another greater or smaller mass. Feelings are aroused which give me the desire to express the reaction of these 'pull forces,' those influences which play with one another; great masses pulling smaller masses, each subject in some degree to the other's power. . . .*

---

[4] *Landscape, Delaware County,* a painting made at home the same year, was subsequently presented to the Metropolitan Museum by Albert E. Gallatin.

"While these powers are at work pushing, pulling, sideways, downwards, upwards, I can hear the sound of their strife and there is great music being played.

"And so I try to express graphically what a great city is doing. Within the frames there must be a balance, a controlling of these warring, pushing, pulling forces. This is what I am trying to realize. But we are all human."

The catalogue for which Marin composed this "explanation" of his artistic intention lists twenty-eight paintings: fifteen views of Fifth Avenue, Broadway, the Brooklyn Bridge, the Woolworth Building, and the Hudson River; six Berkshire landscapes from the Egremont trip with the aunts; six papers from the visit to the Adirondacks with his fiancée; and the honeymoon picture, *Great Falls, Potomac.* The two prevailing aspects of his art now appeared in sharp contrast: the sensitive, lyrical description of nature's outward appearance and the dynamic drama of conflicting pictorial forces, both urban and natural. The ultimate drama of ocean and shore awaited the next year's revelation.

Two of the 1912 paintings of Manhattan Island caught the eye of James Huneker, who conducted a department called "The Seven Arts" in the magazine *Puck,* a sprightly illustrated weekly review of the period. He placed one, *Fifth Avenue,* on the cover of the issue of March 21, 1914, over the caption, "As It Looks to a Leader of the Post-Impressionists." The buildings lining the avenue were bent down to meet over a thick flow of traffic; the color, washed on in blocks and broad strokes, in the manner of *London Omnibus,* was kept down to low-keyed tones of blue and violet. The other, *Woolworth Building,* appeared in Huneker's pages in the issue of April 25, 1914. The Tower, calmer here than was usual, rose in a white column between exciting events in the foreground and sky. Benjamin de Casseres wrote the caption, which called attention to Marin's "luminous humor," a term which has all too rarely appeared in the critical literature.[5] These were almost the last of the pictures to retain the charming but rather old-fashioned transparent tonalities from the Seine River washes in conjunction with the new graphic style.

The art event of the season, the celebrated International Exposition of Modern Art—the so-called Armory Show—occurred at the Sixty-ninth Regiment Armory in February, just after the close of Marin's exhibition. Coming at a time when Rosa Bonheur, Bouguereau, and Alma-Tadema

---

[5] Paul Rosenfeld, in "The Marin Show," *New Republic* (February 26, 1930) pp. 48-50, speaks of Marin's humor as that of "a brother to Emily Dickinson."

were fetching staggering prices, and American taste had in no case advanced appreciably beyond Daubigny and Corot, the Armory Show split the art world of New York into fragments. Arthur B. Davies, Ernest Lawson, and Maurice Prendergast, among the ash-can painters, and Walt Kuhn and others of their younger disciples, had compiled the list of artists whose works were to be borrowed: three hundred artists lending more than a thousand paintings and sculptures, with most of the foreign exhibits chosen in Europe by the astute Walter Pach, a man of taste and discernment who knew everybody in Paris. The lists included Cézanne, Matisse and the *Fauves,* Vincent van Gogh, and some post-impressionist cubists along with their impressionist forebears. There were seven distinct racial sections. The best of the Germans was Lehmbruck, the sculptor. The most famous French picture was Marcel Duchamp's *Nude Descending the Staircase.* Marin's paintings of the Woolworth Tower (Plate 10) were shown in the American section beside the works of ash-can realists, imitative impressionists, and two or three other American painters who belonged to no category.

The show was important to Marin, not because it now put him in touch with the dominant figures of artistic Europe, as was the case with John Sloan,[6] but because the new works of art widened the region in which an American artist could move with freedom and confidence. The professional freedom which Stieglitz guaranteed to his artists, within his small, lively range, was accorded more liberally elsewhere after the Armory Show: as witnessed, for example, by Monet's success in the auctions in the war years that followed. (Marin received, on the other hand, little comfort at home. The irreverent Sarah Shaw—in whom, it is true, reverence was afterwards generated by substantial success—was overheard to remark that Mr. Cass Gilbert's Tower, in Marin's rendition, looked like a clam with bent neck.)

In the summer of 1913, after the spring months in Brooklyn, the Marins, richer by $3,000 from the spring exhibition, went to Castorland, on the Black River in Lewis County, New York, where they made friends with the well-to-do hook-and-eye Baptists who owned the rich dairies in that rolling green countryside. ("Throw away everything interesting about a Quaker and you have an Anni Baptist," wrote Marin to Stieglitz.)[7] They tramped mile after mile, with picnic basket and easel, to find motifs for Marin's first batch of large oil paintings on canvas. Never exhibited and forgetfully dated as of 1912 at some later time, the six Castorland paintings which remain in the artist's possession (two of the series went to Mrs. Shaw,

---

[6] John Sloan, *Gist of Art* (New York, 1939), p. 15.

[7] *Letters of John Marin,* letter to Stieglitz, Castorland, New York, September 10, 1913.

Mrs. Marin's sister) recall the rapid attack of the Palisades series, in the years before Paris, when Marin's style began to take shape in the cold winter weather.

Thinly painted in light colors on unprepared canvas, with unpainted surface left standing for white, these pictures, if people had been able to see them, might have foretold much of what was to come. Granting that Marin's sometimes cryptic symbols were already acknowledged, there is a "real" clump of maple trees (say) in some farmer's sugarbush. But there is also an uncommon amount of "playing around"; for whereas, when giving a motif a various handling with transparent wash, one had to make, at the least, two separate versions, there was time enough with the oil colors to treat more than one aspect of the motif on the one canvas surface. So one of the prevailingly lyrical paintings shows some of its forms "nailed down" with bold strokes of dark pigment, while in yet another, a group of fantastic hemlocks is built up in stitches of color against a "real" background.

Marin was happy at Castorland. It was the kind of big, rolling terrain that he liked to explore: a piece of country providing "fixed ports" for the eye of an artist.[8] Before the summer was over, he had used up, besides the eight canvas stretchers, some fifty sheets of good Whatman paper and was just about ready, he wrote, to paint their "back sides." He advised Stieglitz to "hang these double-faced bastards" on a thousand feet of double-faced screen. "Have the screen set up along the middle of Fifth Avenue," he said, "and await my coming." [9]

He spent many sociable hours with the people who lived in the region: with a friend called Jim Bassett, who, although crippled and ill, seemed to go on living out of pure cussedness; with Old Man Linstruth, bent over double, his face the color of his worn hat and breeches; and pathetic Joe Thompson, not giving up to the coming cash-in, but kindling always, from his broken-down pallet, at the talk of deer runways and trout streams. Marin wrote home of Mike Bowman, who buried his wives—so the neighbors said—under thick slabs of stone to keep them permanently and well out of sight; and of Werner, the milkman, who sang church tunes from Moody and Sankey while he watered his milk. "Pretty fine people, take them all together," said Marin. They were the kind of people he felt easy with.

When the Marins returned to New York from the country that autumn, they moved into the two upper floors of a three-story brick house at the

---

[8] *Letters of John Marin,* letter to Stieglitz, Castorland, New York, July 22, 1913.
[9] *Ibid.*

northeast corner of Twenty-eighth Street and Fourth Avenue—the property
of a newspaper baron who sometimes dropped around to visit the ground
floor of the premises. The studio at the top of the house was lighted by
a row of opaque bull's-eye windows which gave just enough light for work
on the etchings, of which there were nine in that year: including new views
of the Brooklyn Bridge, one of which *New Republic* issued in a subscribers'
edition pulled from a steel facing,[10] and the Woolworth Building (Plate
11), in which sky and tower and city square revolve in a tempest of movement which must have caused Mr. Cass Gilbert, the architect, some further moments of alarm and dismay.

During the winter of 1913–1914, Stieglitz invited scores of his friends
to write testimonials for an issue of *Camera Work* to be entitled "What is
291?" [11] The response was unequal. Some replies had rather more to say
about Marin than about the gallery in general. Thus Charles Daniel, a
formerly conservative dealer, wrote that his first visit to a Marin exhibition had been an important event in his life. It had turned him away
from safe, conventional painting into new paths. Henry McBride wrote
engagingly about Marin's silent, late-afternoon visits to "291": "John Marin
always impresses me as one who is here 'upon a secret errand,' like the
people in the Walter Pater sketches," he said. Marin—somewhat ungram-
matically—made his own contribution: "The place is guarded," he wrote,
halfway down the page of a one-page poem,

<blockquote>
well guarded it
by He—who jealously guards
its innocence, purity, sincerity
subtly guarded it
so that—it seems—not guarded at all
no tyrant he—yet tyrant of tyranny
so shout—we who have felt it
we who are of it
its past—its future
this place
what place?
Oh Hell   291
</blockquote>

Marin discovered Maine in that shattering year of the German *Auf-
marsch* on Belgium: and finding Maine, found his spiritual home. His letters to Stieglitz disclose him, ecstatic in hardship, at Westpoint, a village

<hr>

[10] *John Marin*, Museum of Modern Art Catalogue, No. 102 in the Benson check-list.
[11] July, 1914.

32

near Small Point Beach, fifteen miles south of Bath and due east of Portland across Casco Bay. During August and September he lived in a five-dollar shack on a ledge of rock which, at high tide, was only fifteen feet from the water. "To go anywheres, I have to row, row, row," he wrote to Stieglitz. "Pretty soon I expect the well will give out and I'll then be even obliged to row for water, and as I have to make water colors—to Hell with water for cooking, washing, and drinking." [12] He lived on berries and fish —Stieglitz having advised him to "concentrate on the bread and forget the butter" [13]—and sailed out to Ragged Island and Wallace's Head with his wife and the Haskells, "Father, Mother, and Kid," in a boat which was forever showing her bottom. Ernest Haskell, the etcher, a handsome, broad-shouldered, brown-eyed athlete, risked the lives of all his crew in rough seas more than once, in search of a motif; and to make matters worse, Mrs. Haskell used to frighten her neighbors by putting up sail on a small cockle-shell and setting out into storms.

Haskell, writing a piece about Marin eight years later, recalled the meeting in Westpoint. [14] He had first seen Marin in Paris, at the Dôme, early in 1910, and began to know him, he wrote, at "291" not long after. Marin "cared for what Cézanne stood for—clean emotions," Haskell said. "My admiration grew and grew, even before I discovered the Marin I now know." He sold milk to the painter, wishing all the while that he could give it to him in exchange for the good conversation—which, on Marin's part, was as "selective," he thought, as the paintings.

Haskell used to see Marin climb out onto a limb of a tree in front of his shack, high over the water. Gripping the limb with his knees, his sketching board resting precariously over forked branches, Marin would paint in a fury of ambidexterity, somehow giving off the impression that it was the most natural thing in the world to paint with two hands while straddling the outthrusting limb of a tree. He painted and fished with sincerity, Haskell said, as though he *believed* in fishing and painting. And when they went sailing together, Marin extracted the "essence of sailing" from his transparent paints.

Marin often rowed out to explore a particularly wild offshore island —the island he bought the next year and called Marin Island (Plate 12). He painted spasmodically, for he was upset by the war. Some of his cronies crossed the Atlantic in August to fight; Edward Steichen had turned his gardens at Giverny into burial grounds for the French military. Further-

---

[12] *Letters of John Marin,* letter to Stieglitz, Westpoint, Maine, August 7, 1914.
[13] Paul Rosenfeld, "John Marin's Career," *New Republic* (April 14, 1937), p. 291.
[14] *The Arts,* Vol. II, No. 4, January, 1922, pp. 201-2.

more, Mrs. Marin was pregnant and there wasn't much money at hand. Still, Marin spent day after day studying the sea and the shore. There were wonderful evergreens on the coast . . . "the more beautiful in their last throes when that wonderful parasite moss begins creeping upwards and along the branches—here and there a green piece holding out and then lo, they are in their death clothes, beautiful, wonderful, death wraps." [15] Intent upon his first protracted vision of the sea, since his homeward voyage from Europe, he was inspired to invent his first symbols for seascape.

Since, as we have observed in an earlier chapter, all painting from nature is really symbolic—pictorial forms of whatever degree of "reality" only standing for natural forms—the chief *formal* difference between academic painting and modern painting as practiced by Marin is that whereas the academic painter uses traditional symbols of representation, the modern painter has always felt free to create his own symbols. Cézanne, as Marsden Hartley saw,[16] spent his whole life inventing for himself the new "terms," or symbols, which would best express his understanding of nature: symbols based on the cylinder, the sphere, and the cone.[17]

Marin's new symbols for trees, waves, and rocks were in turn like new coins; the public had to learn their denomination by heart, so to speak, before it could use them for visual currency. The green triangle for pine, the round spot for maple, the polyhedron for rock, the waved line or zigzag for water, and the improvised slash of color for sky may be compared to Chinese characters in the days when those symbols were really pictorial, not yet stylized. And like the Chinese characters, Marin's symbols, less arbitrarily mathematical than Cézanne's, were intended as a means of visual communication between limner and public—the assumption having been made that the public would learn them.

When Marin's work began to get crabbed, as it often did towards the end of a summer, it was because more or less recognizable symbols for natural forms were sometimes arranged in a kind of pictorial counterpoint against purely abstract symbols of a theoretical order: a symbol for boat, for example, set in an arbitrary rectangle. The pictures which usually pass for "typical" Marins have this interplay; they are comparable, to continue our figure, to supposititious Chinese poems composed both of the ancient pictorial characters and their more formal equivalents.

That Marin had begun to play deliberate tricks with reality for plastic

---

[15] *Letters of John Marin*, letter to Stieglitz, Westpoint, Maine, September 16, 1914.

[16] *Adventures in the Arts* (New York, 1921), pp. 30-36.

[17] *Paul Cézanne: Letters*, letter to Emile Bernard, Aix-en-Provence, April 15, 1904, p. 233 (incorrectly numbered CXLVII for CLXVII).

C. *On Morse Mountain, Small Point, Maine, 1928 (water color)*

effect is shown not only in one or two paintings he made in 1914 but also in a letter to Stieglitz: "Nature's arrangements are much finer . . . than my fine studio arrangements. . . . But that don't mean that on your canvas you cannot use these great natural foundlings and juggle and mold and play to your heart's content." [18]

The exhibition of the 1914 water colors at "291" in February, 1915, turned up dissident views of the jugglings and moldings as well as defenders. The New York *Herald* reviewer may be quoted as reporting as follows:

> John Marin, one of the first of American extremists, is show-ing forty-seven of his works in the Gallery, #291, Fifth Avenue. Some of them are disjointed dabs of pure color on white ground, designed to be suggestions of landscapes, and some are views of skyscrapers, their sides bent in impossible directions and their skies apparently full of the suspended debris of dynamite explo-sion. The exhibition makes good for the new art cult, but only the initiated and the faithful can get anything out of it except a bored feeling. This style of art is now about the most common thing in the world.[19]

The size of the 1915 exhibition may excite some reader's wonder. It was not a usual thing for Stieglitz to hang pictures twice, except at the very occasional retrospective showings of the works of his artists; and yet he could muster as many as forty-seven Marin items over the space of one year. According to the records of Miss Rosalind Irvine, secretary of the Amer-ican Art Research Council, Marin made no fewer than sixty-eight paint-ings in 1914. And there may have been more: for no records were kept in either gallery or studio. Marin's first year in Maine was his most prolific year to date. Miss Irvine's photographic records show sixty-three paintings for 1910, a year charged with the excitement of the Tyrolese visit and the return to New York. Nineteen hundred and eleven, a year of reaction, pro-duced very few pictures, eleven on record; 1912 shows fifty-five; 1913 shows forty. Until the completion of the Council's *catalogue raisonné,* one can only conjecture that above the already photographed total of nearly a thou-sand identified oils and water colors, up to 1942, there may be around six hundred additional paintings: for Marin thinks he may have averaged forty pieces a year since 1908. . . .[20]

---

[18] *Letters of John Marin,* letter to Stieglitz, Westpoint, Maine, September 16, 1914.
[19] March 1, 1915. Reprinted in *291.*
[20] Miss Irvine generously supplied the biographer with these figures in a letter of December 18, 1947.

Before leaving Westpoint in the autumn of 1914, the Marins had engaged for next season a large, square cottage at the old Alliquippa House near Small Point Beach, across the cove from their cottage at Westpoint. Surrounded by the usual cluster of Maine camps and cottages, the hotel was filled in the summer with the wives and children of shipbuilders from Bath, bankers from Boston, and college professors from the New England towns: not Marin's sort of people at all, one would think, remembering his Castorland cronies, but perhaps they represented the kind of orderly living that would be conducive to painting, once an otherwise wantless man could afford it. Secure for next year, the Marins went back to New Jersey to stay with Miss Jenny and Miss Lelia Currey until it was time for Mrs. Marin to go to the Woman's Hospital, New York City, where John Marin IV, the only child of the couple, was born in November.

That was a lively winter at "291," for Alfred Stieglitz was planning a new periodical to exploit modern art. Christened *291*, and introduced to the public in the midst of March winds, the new publication appeared in the form of poster-like sheets of folded cardboard, printed with Dadaist decorations and text which illustrated the genius of such foreign celebrities as Braque and Picasso and such native talents as Marin and Walkowitz. The May issue reprinted, with satirical accent, the New York *Herald*'s unfriendly diatribe against Marin, while the June number, featuring Picabia's drawing of the *Fille Née sans Mère,* bore a black and blue cover in which Marin was clearly trying, with commendable sportsmanship, to enter into the spirit of a fantastic jest. To Marin's relief, the periodical was forgotten, save by thoughtful collectors, after twelve impish issues.

Upon taking possession of the hotel cottage at Small Point, in July, 1915, Marin bought his island with half of the sum of $2,000 which Stieglitz, expressing the hope that the money would see him through the next couple of years, was able to give him from the sale of pictures in the preceding season. Rowing out to the island for fishing and painting, Marin tried to forget the grim facts of war, as he shows in his letters—along with the hated invasion of "291" by African art, through Picasso; but he never could build a camp there, as he planned. The island lacked water. Yet he felt, after all, that he had got a good thing for his money, as he tried to explain to his Aunt Jenny Currey, who paid a visit to Small Point that summer to help take care of the baby. For he went back to New York, he believes, with more than one hundred new water colors to show for the season; [21] and Mr. John Quinn, the attorney who had only lately presented

---

[21] Miss Irvine informs me that only thirty-nine of these paintings are on photographic record with the American Art Research Council.

to Congress the art dealers' case for the importation of art duty free, gave enough for just three of them to pay for the island.

After another New Jersey winter and spring, spent in part with the aunts, and later, after Aunt Jenny's death, in a rented house in Wee-hawken,[22] the Marins hired a cottage on Echo Lake, Pennsylvania, in the Kittatinny Mountains, near the Delaware Water Gap. There they spent the summer and fall of 1916, well into November, with Miss Lelia Currey and Richard Currey's two daughters, Lyda and Retta—the cousins who now live near the painter in Cliffside, New Jersey, and, between Mrs. Marin's death and the junior John's marriage, kept an open eye on the bachelor household.

The season was not very prolific of work. It was "blanked-de-blank" hot in August and everyone but the infant was sick. Still, Marin took long hikes through wild country too full of rattlers and copperheads for the women to travel, and visited streams which he first fished and afterwards painted. He fished small-mouth bass, "the finest sport in the world," he wrote Stieglitz. "You first have to know his whereabouts. You have to dress to suit him . . . be wily, firm, not too firm, fast, yet not too fast, slow, not too slow, and sensitive. . . . You have to take a few years off to become a consummate bass fisher." [23] He swam the lake, a mile and a half over and back, and waited for fall and cool weather to come. He cultivated the acquaintance of droll, tobacco-chewing backwoods children, avoiding the "white-duck bunch" of seasonal golfers.

In September he made four "A-1" paintings (Plate 13) and wrote of "floundering along *new lines*." He was getting the feel of the country, and finding mountains, streams, trees, and rocks more sympathetic, as usual, than warlike people. The "floundering," to judge by the paintings, con-sisted in the discovery of further economies, further frugalities with the brush strokes. There is a hint in the letters of his frequently quoted figure of speech from the golf course: "Painting is like golf," he told Stieglitz, on a later occasion. "The fewer strokes I can take, the better the picture." His ideal was a "full, mellow ring to each stroke." [24]

A pair of water colors with a single autumnal motif illustrates the "new lines" of which he was speaking—not for the first time, to be sure,

---

[22] One of the five or six important Marin collections, that of Keith Warner of Ft. Lauderdale, Florida, was assembled around *New York from Weehawken*, a work of that season. This collection of seventeen water colors and seven etchings follows Marin's career from Paris, 1909, to Cape Split, 1941.

[23] *Letters of John Marin*, letter to Stieglitz, Echo Lake, Pennsylvania, September 6, 1916.

[24] *Letters of John Marin*, letter to Stieglitz, Echo Lake, Pennsylvania, September 28, 1916; cf. "Golfer with a Brush," *Time*, January 20, 1947, p. 63.

but with uncommonly striking effect. The first of the pair, still in Marin's possession, is a transcript of a fall panorama in the colors of autumn. The second is a simplification of the motif, a "made" picture, with abstract forms overlaid to cause purely plastic excitement. The second version, in Marin's opinion, remains one of the most significant pictures of his entire career. It was the first time, he modestly felt, that he had "played" with a subject and come richly out with something that was clearly the expression of painterly intellect rather than an impression of his feeling for nature. His purpose was plainly analogous to one of Renoir's professional objects (after 1880), though the means were his own: namely, to indicate the architectural structure of nature under the surface appearance, under the fleeting impression. He was not afraid then, as he has not been since, of showing subjective feeling in pictures, but he liked to make sure that the analytic and objective matter was primarily present.

Back in Small Point for the season of 1917, after a winter in the rented house in Weehawken, Marin took a new cottage at the Alliquippa House, now run by a Philadelphia Quaker. He worried that year about the treatment of sky in a seascape—of which the sky almost necessarily occupies at least a third part. Now a sky, except in a thunderstorm or at sunset, he reasoned, is not very lively. On a lucky day you might pick up a mackerel sky or some tufted cirrus; but more often than not, the sky is not the chief organ of nature's sentiment, as Constable called it, but a blank, empty wall in back of a landscape. So what do you do? If you are Marin, you put something to see in the sky; or you merely show, in the most economical way, that it's there. If there are unformed clouds, you can pull them together. If nothing is there, you can paint in patches of color—any color you like—to make the blank wall exciting. You can put in blue or gray symbols, or possibly red or yellow (whatever you need to round out your complement), and let them stand for the sky. Then you will not be in danger of boring the spectator by showing him a third of your paper covered with robin's-egg blue or turquoise.

Marin now had his full list of symbols in shape, and having thus created his language, he began to master his handling of landscape. Things that had seemed big for speech now seemed little, he was able to say. Once bowled over by nature, now he could bend it. He could reduce his vision to the size of the paper. Yet, he felt, he had not "got fresh" with nature. Let him who is tempted to betray nature's magnitude, he suggested to Stieglitz, try to bridge the Atlantic or level the world's highest mountains.[25]

---

[25] *Letters of John Marin*, letter to Stieglitz, Small Point, Maine, July 3, 1917.

Having discovered his powers, he was able to sound the praises of Small Point in wartime letters that read like Walt Whitman poems:

My dear Stieglitz:

There was a time about two weeks gone when I should have written to you. Then the mind was, if anything, clearer. Now it's hot. . . . But there are degrees, and how much hotter other places in this poor old scrapping world. And what are they scrapping about? . . .

We up here get but few glimpses of the outer world . . . a fish boat looks big, a sail boat looms up, the eagles soaring overhead are big, or is not their bigness a something of the imagination. As, if you were floundering, how big a plank would look. As, if in the wilderness lost, what a little light would mean. As, in a city, one light means little or nothing. As, in a world harbor, the insignificance of one little boat. . . .

A native to show the traveler the way.

A pilot to steer the boat through, knowing the channels.

Can you trust him, blurts out this awful word—trust.

Ignorance, stupidity, knavishness, selfishness. No.

Kindliness. Kindliness and intelligence. Yes.

Until then, we will have no peace, no rest. . . .

And one might go on, talk of art in its different forms. As to whether in the tearing up, the making of new paths. As to how much new road, real road, will be made. . . .

I want an answer to the question, a real answer, a true answer, the only answer. Who can give it?

There is an answer, there must be the Only answer.

And that, I suppose, is why the whole of nature scraps, unconsciously, periodically scraps. . . . The beast cries out, one of its answers is food, food of some kind. When we are no longer hungry, no longer cry for food, death comes. . . .

I have just been in for a swim and feel better. The water delicious, the sands to the touch of the feet. Big shelving wonderful rocks, hoary with enormous hanging beards of sea weed, carrying forests of evergreen on their backs. The big tides come in, swift, go out swift. . . .

Wonderful days.

Wonderful sunset closings.

Good to have eyes to see, ears to hear the roar of the waters.

Nostrils to take in the odors of the salt sea and the firs.

Fish fresh, caught some myself.

John Marin

Berries to pick. . . .
Big flying eagles.
The solemn restful beautiful firs.
The border of the sea.
Good night.
My island looks tantalizingly beautiful.
My boy is brown and well, full of life. My wife is brown and well.
I am brown and well. . . .

Your friend, Marin
Got the two checks all right, many thanks.
Nibbling at work! [26]

The checks of which Marin writes had answered the vexing question of his immediate domestic economy; for after the season's exhibitions of the Stieglitz group—Marsden Hartley, Rabelaisian Abraham Walkowitz, S. Macdonald Wright, Georgia O'Keeffe—the "Little Galleries" had been quietly closed.

---

[26] *Letters of John Marin,* letter to Stieglitz, Small Point, Maine, July 31, 1917.

The Critical Years

1918—Summer, 1925

"YOU ARE LUCKY . . . IN HAVING A SUMMER PLACE YOU CAN sort of call home," Marin wrote in 1918 to Stieglitz, who occupied his father's country place on Lake George.[1] The Marins had no home at all. They had abandoned the Weehawken house, at this critical time, for the sake of economy; and when the summer of 1918 arrived, the Alliquippa Hotel was filled up before they got around to applying for a cottage. Marin took his wife and son to Rowe, Massachusetts, a few miles northeast of Zoar Station on the Deerfield River, in Franklin County, where he had heard he could rent a small hunting lodge for five dollars a month. Set in stupid country among run-down dairy farms, the place was three dreary miles from the nearest market and a mile and a half from safe milk for young John. The closest "beautiful view" was also about three miles away. There was lots of hiking to do for a man who had his heart set on painting.

The trout fishing was fair, so Marin went fishing—although he had never been, by first choice, a trout fisherman. The worst thing about fishing a trout stream, he said, is that people expect you to fish trout downstream, whereas he preferred traveling upstream. He planted a kitchen garden, picked mushrooms and berries, and cut up dead fruit trees for the fire. He missed the ocean, but when he had time for his painting he made the most of the pictorial values the countryside offered. He composed several tender wash drawings of wide-eyed, red-eared young Ayrshire bull calves whose dams grazed near his cottage, and painted the round hills of the district, the Hoosac Mountains, in unconventional patterns of color.

The trite shapes of things in the Hoosacs did not oblige him to draw and compose in structural form; they were not, in any true sense, subject matter for delineation. Hence he made essays—of which at least twelve have survived—in big sweeping masses, imperceptibly drawn, and in thin, whimsical color, such as pale pink for the hills and pale green for the sky. Sometimes he used those two hues alone, sometimes put down pale blue. Most of these washes look rather vaporish and somewhat unearthly; yet among them there are examples in which the metaphysician is kept down to earth

---

[1] *Letters of John Marin,* letter to Stieglitz, incorrectly dated September 2, 1915, and printed with the 1915 letters.

by the poet. If the more theatrical papers experimented with the place-
ment of color on white—to give it freedom to move in and space to be
seen in—the series concluded with a smashing down-to-earth autumn landscape, a reversal of the painter's usual process of painting objectively and
then "playing around."

Wrought in months of torment from war, from insecurity, from un-
congenial surroundings—the mangled and cut-over woods made Marin rest-
less—the season's work as a whole did not please him. "I don't know what
the future holds in living or anything else," he told Stieglitz.[2] Having struck
off from the main line of his progress, he worried about methods and
motifs. What method is best? What problem is most important? These
were the questions he asked himself as he spent long hours analyzing from
memory the work of old masters whose paintings he knew. He would have
liked to retreat from the world which enclosed him. "Blessed be the restricted herd," he wrote, thinking of the neighboring dairies. "All of us
who can be, are fence jumpers." [3]

It was not until the first part of October, when he "went to bed with
the quietness of green and wakened up to the blaze of yellows and reds,"
that he was happy again. The strong colors got at him as the soft shapes of
the hills had been unable to do. He borrowed a gun and went hunting;
began to wish he could stay in the woods for the winter, eating apples and
drinking cider out of an old-fashioned jug whose simple shape pleased him.
He hung on until snowfall, to save money. Stieglitz had proved to be able,
even in war time, to dispose of a painting or two, but there was not enough
income to live on in town—not to speak of hiring a studio where he could
hang up his work for contemplating in winter. (That was the year he took
a dollar apiece from the Biltmore Hotel for a large batch of etchings and
accepted Mrs. Shaw's offer of a room for the winter in her house in Flatbush. It was the year the war came to an end and relieved a grieving and
sensitive man of his gravest misgivings.)

The particular professional worries of 1918 vanished soon after Marin
reached the Maine coast once more—at Stonington, in 1919. In those days
you reached that harbor town on Deer Isle aboard the Bar Harbor steam-
ers *Baudwell* and *Morse,* out of Rockland, crossing Penobscot Bay past Vin-
alhaven. After the economical winter which Sarah Shaw's kindness afforded,
Marin was able to take a good house looking out on the harbor, "a house

---

[2] *Letters of John Marin,* the letter incorrectly dated September 2, 1915.
[3] *Letters of John Marin,* letter to Stieglitz, Cyrus (editorial error for Rowe), Massachusetts,
October 5, 1918.

for meals, a house for sleep, a house for warmth, a house for the weary." [4] There was a reproduction of a drawing by Raphael, a large female nude, on a wall of the privy. "If you want to find art in this country, you must look for it there," Marin said. (He came to hate the drawing for its perfection and smugness.)

It was a saving of time to be in touch with a village again, to buy milk from near neighbors and groceries just down the street: though of course one still fished and hunted and went berry picking, with pleasure, to supply the home larder. One missed, that first season at Stonington, the intimacy of the small coves and beaches at Small Point, yet one came in the end to appreciate the more various movement in the Stonington harbor. The fishermen still hauled lobster from sailboats, and there were scores of small islands to break the flat surface of sea. "It seems that Old Man God, when he made this part of the Earth, just took a shovel full of islands and let them drop," Marin wrote.[5] They made the sea sparkle.

He hired a power boat to search out new motifs, spending day after day on the water. The earliest Stonington pictures carried on the rather unsatisfactory innovations from Rowe, the round masses of the Hoosac hills giving way to angular patterns which stood for Maine rocks, while blue trees replaced the green sky in the quest for pictorial freedom. Looking, in New York, at those transcribed forms, separated by wide spaces of untinted paper, Stieglitz—according to Marin—was to mutter "Gee whiz!" But inside of a month, the painter was back in good form, recording impressions and "playing around" in his most vigorous style.

When Marin began to feel more at home in the district—the people, he said, looked like Marsden Hartley, the blue-eyed, Yankee-faced painter who came from Lewiston—he settled down to make the acquaintance of neighbors as well as their landscape. The fisherman from whose cow barn he fetched home the milk told old tales of the sea in a voice so enchanting that his visitor often sat with him late into the night. Occasional painters turned up to spend a few weeks in the place. They gazed at the ocean over their palettes, Marin reported, but it seemed to him that their brushes never followed their eyes. They painted what they had seen in old seascapes. They looked at chickens walking about in a barnyard and then painted them hopping. The great masters, Marin noted, "didn't make their chickens to hop." [6]

Still, the visiting artists seemed to sell their pictures quite handily.

---

[4] *Letters of John Marin,* letter to Stieglitz, Stonington, Maine, September 1, 1919.
[5] *Letters of John Marin,* letter to Stieglitz, Stonington, Maine, July 1, 1919.
[6] *Letters of John Marin,* letter to Stieglitz, Stonington, Maine, October (no date), 1919.

Marin, painting from the directest of visions, therefore wondered whether he might not be too much of a realist. (Noyes, the druggist, asked him if he finished his pictures at home in New Jersey, so a body could tell what they represented!) There had come in, during that summer of his fiftieth year, a substantial check for one picture—close to $1,000—but there was not yet enough settled income for three people to live well on through the winter. Marin felt that deceit and hypocrisy lay side by side in their bed and brought forth success, while truthfulness lacked an equally fruitful partner. Restlessness caused his work to fall off in volume:

My dear Stieglitz: (he wrote on August 15, 1919)

Today I am in one "Hell of a mood."

I did something I rather like, a disorderly orderly sort of a thing. I am up on my haunches. I don't know just what to do.

I sort of want to raise Hell in my stuff and don't know how to do it properly.

Feel like tearing things to pieces. . . .

In my present mood don't like anything much.

Want to be crazy. . . .

To paint disorder under a big order.

Smugness.

When is one not smug?

Is it when one is tossed about and tosses, being played with and playing? Maybe that's a thrust at it, a stab at it.

Assuredness.

Cock-surity.

Honors.

Ter Hell with Honors.

Ditto old masters, young masters, all kinds of masters. Hurray for all things that come to grief, that slobber, that come a cropper. The Smugs roam the earth—no they stay put. The Smugs start all the trouble, they Exasperate.

It takes nerve not to be smug and no one has nerve enough. Nature just loves nerve.

Today I am an apostle of the crazy, but Damit, it's got to be a caged crazy, otherwise it would butt into another crazy. Then you have destruction. So. There you have the ideal humanity, crazy humanity, each in his little cage.

That would be a show.

Maybe that's what God is waiting for, for all the world to become

44

crazy. Then he'll crate them and put a label tag on each and ship them. So that's what each one should live for, look forward to, religiously, becoming with all one's heart and soul and strength crazy—crazy all, but it's a long way off.

The World is too full of the Smugs.

So, Weep for poor God.

So long.

Good night.

Marin.

P.S. This is one Smug letter all right.

Hoping, nevertheless, to complete an average number of paintings, Marin stayed on at Stonington, with time out for a brief visit to Small Point (Plate 14), until the day before Christmas, when he sailed out with his wife and small son in a lobster smack which tacked its way through a snowstorm to the harbor at Rockland. After spending the rest of the winter in Union Hill with faithful Aunt Lelia Currey, the Marins moved to Cliffside, New Jersey, where they bought one of three nearly identical two-story stucco houses (No. 243) on Clark Terrace, a shady street which travels downhill from the main thoroughfare, Anderson Avenue, towards the Hudson at a point roughly across from Grant's Tomb. Today a built-up, commonplace town containing rows of houses and shops with false fronts, Cliffside then was composed of a few scattered cottages in good, clear country. A few minutes' walk or a short ride on a bicycle would carry a painter into paintable territory. Marin knocked out a partition between two upstairs rooms at the back of his house, overlooking a tulip tree, and made a permanent studio. Except for the winter in the newspaper baron's apartments on West Twenty-eighth Street and a few months in Marsden Hartley's old studio on West Fourteenth, near the Ninth Avenue "El," he had not had a winter workroom of his own since his marriage. His winter production now began to increase.

A retrospective show of fifty water colors had been hung at the Daniel Gallery, 2 West Forty-seventh Street, in April, the pictures ranging from the Tyrolese series of 1910 to the Stonington, 1919, papers—including twenty-five pictures from the summer at Rowe. The hill pictures, incorrectly labeled Hoosic for Hoosac, bore such titles as *Mountain Forms*, numbered from one to six, and *Mountain Tops*, in three versions. It was this show which brought Marin his first liberal patron, Ferdinand Howald, a shy, modest, broad-shouldered engineer from Columbus, Ohio.

Howald (b. 1854) had been reared to such a taste for art by his mother that he rarely spoke of anything else save in short, bristling syllables; and

45

having made his fortune in the West Virginia coal region, he took up collecting shortly after the turn of the century. Resolving to buy only contemporary works of art, and of these only such as gave him personal pleasure, he looked first to Paris, where, within fifteen years, he acquired the work of Braque, Derain (seven paintings), Juan Gris, Matisse (four paintings), Picasso, and Vlaminck (three paintings). In New York he bought examples of some of the American realists: Arthur B. Davies (three paintings), William Glackens (four paintings), Ernest Lawson (eight paintings), George Luks (three paintings), Maurice Prendergast (sixteen paintings). Then he met Alfred Stieglitz, who showed him how to find pleasure in Demuth (thirty-one paintings), Macdonald Wright (seven paintings), Marsden Hartley (fifteen paintings), Abraham Walkowitz, Max Weber, and finally, Marin, from whom, in the space of four years, he bought thirty-two water colors.

Of the twenty-eight Marins in the Howald Collection, as presented to the Columbus Gallery of Fine Arts in April, 1931, two years before the death of the donor, seventeen were bought in one season at the Daniel Gallery. The others were added from various sources before 1925: 1910 the earliest and 1923 the latest date represented.[7] The sales paid for the new house in Cliffside.

It was also this exhibition which inspired Marsden Hartley to write his essay, "Some American Water-Colorists," which appeared the next year in his book, *Adventures in the Arts,* a volume dedicated by the author to Stieglitz. The essayist briefly traced Marin's course up to 1919, from the "earliest Turner tonalities," through "Whistlerian vagaries"—Charles Bittinger challenged the Whistlerian reference as inaccurate in respect to Marin's warm, definite color—on to "American definiteness." Marin had found himself, Hartley said, in New York and Maine. He also wished to say, he explained, "that Marin produces the liveliest, handsomest wash that is producible or that has ever been accomplished in the field of water-color painting." (In another essay in the same volume, Hartley observed that Winslow Homer, as compared to Marin, had perhaps more infallibly said what he wanted to say, but Homer's reach, he thought, was less lofty.)[8]

If Marin showed any defects, Hartley felt, they were defects of virtuosity —of high execution and polish—not of skill and intention. Yet he saw that Marin, like the Chinese painters, understood the "majesty of the limitations"

---

[7] Four pictures were given to Mr. Howald's niece, Mrs. Robert Shawan, of Columbus, Ohio, to whom I am indebted for a biographical memoir communicated by telephone. For a comprehensive view of the Howald Collection, see "American Collections—No. 1," by Forbes Watson, *The Arts,* Vol. VIII, No. 2, August, 1925, pp. 65-95.

[8] *Adventures in the Arts* (New York, 1921), p. 44.

of the transparent medium and rarely pushed it too far. There was just the least possibility, he supposed, in a period dominated by the posthumous fame of Cézanne's great innovations, that the "exactitude of emotion" in Marin's work might be thought to lack its "precise ratio of thought"; for Cézanne had taught that intellectual matters like spacial existence and spacial relationships were the chief ingredients of a work of art. (He never worked, as we saw, from the first emotional impulse following impact from a new situation.) In the long run, however, Hartley thought that Marin's surpassing naturalness more than made up for any unbalance between sensuality and intellectual calm.

C. Lewis Hind was able to trace, he believed, Marin's ten-year development from "sense to inspiration," akin to Turner's history as expounded by Ruskin. Nature had led Marin, he found, both "deeper and deeper" and "higher and higher": so that he had become at once more profound and abstract (i.e., theoretical).[9] Marin's deepest intention, as I have here tried to describe it, had already been sufficiently realized for a watchful critic to spot it exactly.

In the summer of 1920 Marin began to look closely at the village of Stonington. "Maybe, having purchased a house, I am kidding myself into an interest in houses," he said.[10] He felt that he was finding his way into his motifs. Already suspicious of interior visions, of psychological painting, as later of surrealism's excessive subjectivities, he clung to nature's realities. He preferred "open-sight vision" to "inner vision" as the more reliable guide to the artist. Yet, being by nature a mystic—a nontheological mystic—he craved revelation: provided its source could be reached through the senses. One gazed not into one's soul, but straight into nature, as hard as one could; and then nature, acting as the Greek Logos, the divine Word, acted upon the theological mystic, opened the inmost door and introduced the interrogator to the ultimate mysteries. Like the writings of the theological mystics, Marin's words on this subject are not always clearly comprehensible; but it is this kind of supranatural experience of the natural world that the letters of 1920 most certainly hint at.

The sight of a schooner looming up under full sail as he lay off in his boat in Stonington harbor on October 7, 1920, filled him with indescribable wonder. It was a "thing of life, changing with every second," he said,[11] and the twenty drawings he made caught the changing life of the ship. In identifying himself, so to speak, with the schooner, he felt he had got inside his

---

[9] C. Lewis Hind, *Art and I* (London, 1921), pp. 176 ff.
[10] *Letters of John Marin,* letter to Stieglitz, Stonington, Maine, September 14, 1920.
[11] *Letters of John Marin,* letter to Stieglitz, Stonington, Maine, October 7-October 12, 1920.

motif. Hence—if the difference can be made to be felt—he believed that the drawings were not merely subjective impressions of objective reality but records of revelations received through objective experience. The distinction may be hard to conceive, but an understanding of Marin is inseparably bound to this mystical side of his make-up.

Having made, then, this frankly religious accommodation of his own spirit to nature's, Marin grew more joyful and bolder. Although he continued to search through his work every day, examining his paintings for errors as a monk searches his conscience, he began to feel confidence in his waxing powers. The exhibition of the 1920 Stonington pictures, at the Daniel Gallery in April, 1921, was full of fresh sparkle. Henry McBride, writing in the May issue of *Dial,* invited the English novelists Arnold Bennett and Somerset Maugham to come to New York to see the new paintings: Bennett having once told reporters that he had come to this country to take a broad look at Winslow Homer. Now it was time, McBride said, to come again to see Marin's shifting skies and turbulent seas which, with their "smashing feeling for harmony," matched Beethoven's music.[12]

It was during the Stonington years that Marin began with some regularity to enclose subject matter with the bold "frames within frames" that his public came to expect and to look for. "When I got what I wanted, I nailed the stuff down in those frames," Marin says. In some of the water colors, he had already "framed" a whole study with a dark band of color to keep it from appearing to slide off the edge of the paper. Now he pointed out, by means of frame with frame, how one part of the whole asserted itself in respect to another. Each tree, island, and ship, or each house in a village, was often, now and later, thus given its pointedly particular place (and particular plane) in the general tension set up in a picture.

After it got about that the self-enclosed pictures were "typical" the collectors all wanted water colors from the Stonington years: although the frame within frame was, broadly speaking, not a typical concept at all. That it is really exceptional an examination of hundreds of consecutively dated paintings has shown me. The interior frame was only one of a number of structural and thematic devices, any two or three of which could produce a "typical" Marin. The introduction of arbitrary forms in the sky was more "characteristic," for instance, in respect to its frequency, than the bands of deep blue

---

[12] Henry Tyrrell, in "American Aquarellists—Homer to Marin," *International Studio* (September, 1921), p. XXXIII, wrote that Marin had "freed himself and his medium forever from earthbound banality," and that a literal landscape from his hand would have been as far removed from its author's element as a political pamphlet from the hand of Shelley. Cf. the more restrained but nonetheless uncompromised view of Thomas J. Craven in *Shadowland* (October, 1921): "In the field of water-color [Marin] has made himself unapproachable."

or black surrounding the sum of a picture or its principal parts. An observant collector in the early twenties might have come thus to feel that it would take at least three paintings to represent Marin's range: a shattering, tumbling, violent view of Manhattan (Plates 10, 15); a Maine seacoast piece with the slashing framework and broad indication of planes (Plates 16, 17, 18); and a lyrical landscape or seascape containing the typical unequal balance—in the former's favor—between what Hartley called the excitement and the calm of research (Plate 14).

The winter of 1920–1921 saw Marin partly crippled with frequent and painful attacks of lumbago, a disorder which has interrupted his work from time to time ever since. It is only in summer, and then not invariably, that he is quite free of it. In the summer after his seventy-fifth birthday, for example, he plunged naked into the frigid Maine waters and spent long days in damp boats with water up to his ankles, impatient still of whatever looked like indulging the flesh: and paid the charges to the lumbar region. But those early rheumatic attacks—no more than the latest—never quite brought his work to a halt. There were several vigorous studies of Manhattan that winter.

In the summer of 1921 the Marins rented their house, which was not yet quite paid for, and went back to Stonington, where they continued to live off the sea and the land. They dug clams and caught fish and ate lobster and crab provided by friends who hauled traps for a living. Mrs. Marin made blueberry muffins and pies and likewise canned fruit to take back to the city. Marin shot duck and rabbit, for the sake of variety, and as he tramped through the woods, learned to distinguish the edible mushrooms. He bought a cheap power boat, the care of which—fixing and caulking and painting and pumping—caused the painting of pictures to take second place in his thoughts. "It leaked like hell," he complained, but he loved it. He wouldn't have traded it for any "blooming yacht" from Bar Harbor. He could land on a beach anywhere in the bay, strip down and bathe, and reflect on the "tremendous, the fathomless, the wondrous ocean." And in spite of the old boat's demands, he managed to use up a good deal of his choice Whatman paper in painting some pictures that he liked very much.

Stieglitz asked him to write a catalogue Note for an exhibition of 110 water colors, four oils of Maine and Manhattan, and thirty-one etchings, to be held at the Montross Gallery the following January, and Marin produced "Here It Is," a small essay with a whimsical Foreword.[13] Like most of his published fragments, it was not very helpful to a precise understanding of its author's paintings, yet it yielded one or two useful comments on the Marin aesthetic.

---

[13] Reprinted in *Manuscripts*, No. 2, March, 1922; and again in the unpaged *Letters of John Marin*, after a letter to Stieglitz, September 11, 1921.

It urged painters to save the identity of their subject matter—thus showing that Marin was not, by intention, really the abstractionist painter that he was then being called.

A round is a round and a square is a square, he maintained, in a parable, and it can change only in size and keep its identity. He had no use for a still life with a table that sloped or a flower vase that would spill. Flatness to him was a function of table, uprightness a function of vases. Whatever else an artist does with his subject matter, he concluded, he cannot be allowed to fool around with its function.

The exhibition evoked a tribute from a fellow painter, Albert E. Gallatin, who wrote that Marin was not only "one of the greatest and most profound artists America has produced," but also the supreme water colorist. It was necessary to "travel back to the ancient Chinese masters," he thought, to find his equal. "Marin has sought not merely to copy nature, to give us literal transcription, after the manner of the Impressionists, but rather to portray an emotion, to 'emphasize nature here, and distort it there, all in harmony with a definite artistic purpose' (I borrow these words from a work on Japanese landscape gardening.). . . . Marin is a visionary, his work, always so beautifully organized and so superb in design, is full of mystery. Emotions are evoked which show him to be a poet with the rapture of Shelley." [14]

The climax of Gallatin's commentary on Marin is reached in a passage from Goethe: "When the artist takes any object from nature, the object no longer belongs to nature; indeed we say that the artist creates the object in that moment, by extracting from it all that is significant, characteristic, interesting, or rather by putting it into a higher value." This, Gallatin thought, was exactly what Marin had done. (One may note, incidentally, in connection with the passage from Goethe, that if there were a term such as "extractionist" in the vocabulary of art history, it would more nearly represent Marin's treatment of nature than the term "abstractionist" ever could.)

Paul Rosenfeld, a subtle detector of nuances, wrote in *Vanity Fair* of the variety of moods in which Marin worked: now tranquil, now frantic, and again with the engaging humor of a "leprechaun," a "sort of boy igniting water-color squibs." [15] The high humor which breaks out all over the letters is visible, as he saw, in much of the painting. Henry McBride compared the "frantic" works to the "craggy books" that Byron liked to break his mind upon.[16]

The four new oil paintings, one from Small Point, one from Deer Isle,

[14] *American Water-Colourists* (Copyright E. P. Dutton & Co., Inc., New York, 1922), pp. 17 ff.
[15] April, 1922, p. 88.
[16] New York *Herald*, Sunday art section, January 29, 1922.

and two from Manhattan, came as a surprise to the critical public. Marin had been painting in oil now and then, ever since 1904, to keep his hand in, but he rarely showed the canvases outside of his studio. He was busy, he now supposes, consolidating his reputation as a water colorist, and the oil paintings, he feared, would confound the public. He was perfectly right. When he showed the four new canvases of 1921, they were either ignored or rejected. Marin had been hard to catch on to, and no one was ready to follow the shift to a medium which expressed a radically different intention.

By no means everybody had as yet "caught on" to the water colors themselves. Reporting on a comprehensive water-color exhibition at the Brooklyn Museum, at which fourteen washes by Marin, dating from 1914 to 1920, occupied an entire end wall, Herbert J. Seligmann said that the people standing in front of them looked either troubled or curious, although a relatively "easy" selection was made from descriptive washes with Debussy-like titles and atmospheric effects of rain, moonlight, and wind. Paul Strand made it clear, however, that the Marin paintings overshadowed the rest. He found no "dead spots" in them: which was more than could be said of Winslow Homer, or of anyone else, in late times, but Cézanne. . . .[17]

Marin's father, John C. Marin, died during that winter in his eighty-fifth year, having affectionately followed his son's career through his fiftieth birthday. A tall, handsome man with a hooked Gallic nose and standing six feet in his middle eighties, the senior Marin had long since retired from business and in late years had gone much with his wife into artistic New York society. He had a fine voice which he displayed to his friends on occasion, Mrs. Marin providing the piano accompaniment, and he kept up his lifelong interest in music and practiced looking at pictures right up to his death. Not long before his last illness, he had written to Stieglitz, from the Hotel Beresford on Central Park West, where the elder Marins made their home in New York, to say that he could never find words to express his appreciation of Stieglitz's interest in John. "I am glad," he related, "that he has responded . . . not only by his ability but also by his loving esteem. He writes he is hard at work and hopes to bring with him work that will show steady progress."[18] He promised to lend out his copy of Hartley's new book, with its tribute to Marin.

Although he had not, for ten years, paid out a regular sum to his son every month, nor arranged to bequeath him the half of his property, he had come to be first unashamed and then proud of the painter, who correspondingly missed his father's friendly and frequent visits to Cliffside. Mrs. Isabel

---

[17] "American Water Colors at the Brooklyn Museum," *The Arts,* December, 1921, pp. 148 ff.

[18] Unpublished letter to Alfred Stieglitz, The Beresford, October 5, 1921. Courtesy of Mrs. Dorothy Norman.

Marin, after the death of her husband, took over the charge, so far as one could with a stepson of fifty, and in March, 1922, saw him through a tonsilectomy to which he subjected himself with the greatest reluctance on the peremptory advice of Alfred Stieglitz's brother, Dr. Leopold Stieglitz. Mrs. Marin wrote to Stieglitz to tell him that John was all right.[19]

On the way back to Stonington for the next summer season (1922), Marin drove his first car, his wife complaining that he drove much too fast and looked out of the window. They made the side trip, fifteen miles of early June quagmire, from Bath to Small Point, where they rowed out to Marin Island with a box of crackers and a small jug of water. They were disappointed thereafter—as Marin was every year—with their first look at Stonington. But after the boat had been tinkered by a giant machinist who played the fiddle and fixed false teeth on the side, the harbor began to look more attractive. Work on the boat and attacks of lumbago having spoiled the month of July, a trip to Bold Island in August brought out the paint cups for a session of work.

Bold Island was a magnificent motif. It rose up all the way round from the water and at its high summit there were ridges of granite where you could sit down and look out over the sea upon Scragg Island, Devil's Island, Camp Island. Granite quarries had augmented the natural rock forms, a century earlier, and gave Marin plenty of chance to play with his symbols for rocks. On Mt. Desert Island, where he visited Arthur B. Carles, the bearded Philadelphia painter who had been one of the boys at Café Dôme in Paris, he painted a thunderstorm breaking over a lake. He saw a big, white-headed eagle shouldering its way through the wind. "That's the bird for me," he told Carles. "Oh, to be bold, when it isn't easy!" The eagle appeared often thereafter in his painting and writing. "I am a shouting, spread-eagled American," he liked to say.[20]

He was working that fall, after Mrs. Marin took John home to Cliffside for school, on an article, "Can a Photograph Have the Significance of Art?" for Stieglitz's luxurious new publication called *Manuscripts*. That short-lived periodical had made its appearance in February as a cooperative enterprise on the part of its authors. The first issue contained Sherwood Anderson's wonderful story, "A Testament," beginning, "I have become an old man and my mother is dead. I live in a town in Ohio. . . ." The second issue reprinted

---

[19] Unpublished letter to Alfred Stieglitz, The Beresford, March 10, 1922. Courtesy of Mrs. Dorothy Norman.

[20] Paul Rosenfeld, echoing Paul Strand in the Brooklyn essay, was to say later that Marin achieved a "sort of absolute painting as American in feeling as Whitman's [poetry] and as simultaneously rough and exquisite." *New Republic* (April 14, 1937), p. 292.

three of Marin's literary productions, "Foreword," "Here It Is," and "Notes (Autobiographical)." For the fourth issue (December, 1922), Stieglitz compiled thirty-one unequally unambiguous answers to his leading question. Marin, very much on the spot, had replied with an involved and a devious "maybe." His letter, however, contains some crabbedly useful reflections on art.

"The painter can create in past, present, and future," Marin wrote. He himself was painting entirely in the present then, but the time was to come when he would rely on the past to enrich present time—the past's function; when he would paint the sea, for example, in a glade in the woods. When he asked, "What is art anyway?", he was no more able than any man of his time to give the right answer; yet he used, for the first time in print, the musical similes which, as later elaborated, must take a permanent place in all talk about Marin. He likened the artist's "instrument" to a musical instrument which must give out the "sing" of the player's life. The record of that "sing" is the work of art. And the song must be pure. Marin humbly felt that up to that time he had not made the pure song he was capable of. But he was forever refining the music he made.

The winter's work in the city was adding up faster now that Marin had his own permanent studio: not that he worked much indoors, except to tinker with oils, but it meant a good deal to have a place to go back to where he could study his outdoor production. October, 1922, found him roaming the Palisades with his paints—until he got a "good big dose" of the poison ivy. He made plans that winter to go farther afield when he got back to Maine, but when the summer of 1923 came around, it proved not so easy to carry them out. It was one thing to cruise around Penobscot Bay with an outboard motor and quite another to transport a car to the mainland on the local ferry, a scow which carried only three cars at a time and took an hour to make the round trip. He did, however, visit Blue Hill on August 13, 1923—"Blue Hill, like the hill of the Japanese Fujiyama." It had character, "enough bare, enough wooded," to make him want to paint a finer blue hill than Blue Hill itself.

The little worldly success that had come to him from the Daniel and Montross exhibitions had in no way inflated his ego. He had many misgivings. He felt handicapped by want of direction, was depressed to find that he still felt at loose ends, at his age. He faced once more the annual problem which had to do with the yearly transition from city to shore. He had every year to find the right track. A man was in a bad way, he confessed, when he got off the track on his way after a drink of plain water. He wanted to paint lots of boats that year, but few boats had come into the harbor. "Last year my gun was not especially loaded for schooners," he said, yet many schooners had put

53

into the bay. This year, on the contrary, he was loaded for schooners, but now they were "mighty few and scarce."[21]

The sudden death of a fisherman friend—up last week and talking and this week three days in his grave—caused him to think much of mortality. "We don't want to die, until nature prepares us for death. Those whom nature has so prepared, don't care. No, they do care to die, have an inclination for it, desire it. . . ." Marin had not yet received his "dope potion" from nature, he said, hence he desired to live and do worthwhile things—"though those worthwhiles may never be." So "to Hell with Walt Whitman's hymn to death, say I. He was already beginning to croak. No man is old until he begins those croakings. Some are born with it, they love to call the work of others *light, airy*. There is plenty of light if you can see it, away down deep in the utmost depths." Trying to shake off this mood of depression, he commanded himself to go down into his depths and haul up the light. Concluding that if Picasso had lately seemed to have lost his direction, Toulouse-Lautrec, at the turn of the century, had managed, through bad times, to keep it, he worked on into the winter over the familiar "Maine stuff." His sense of direction returned to him slowly.

He reflected about that indefinable attribute which we call "quality": "Yesterday I heard a bird singing. Well, I might go down in Africa and hear a lion roar—down the street, the honk of an automobile—down the city, a jazz band. There was quality to the bird's singing, wonderful quality. So in the lion's roar, could be in the honk of the auto, could be in the jazz band. *Quality*. That's what the few of the world will always cry out for, till domesday. I know it. That's one of my convictions if I have any."

A September letter helpfully states another of the plain themes of Marin's aesthetic: the love of subject matter and paint. If you have an intense love for your subject—Marin's subjects were still rocks, trees, houses, and boats—you will try your damndest, he said, to put its essence on paper or canvas. You can transpose, you can play with and around your material, but when you are finished, the picture must have the look of a loved object as revealed to the lover.

Those were high thoughts: perhaps not so well phrased as a philosopher might have phrased them; nevertheless, they were of a lofty philosophical order. The standard was almost too high for mortal man to live up to, hence there were not many new pictures that their author was thoroughly pleased with. It was not often, he thought, that he could nail down the vision to suit him, in spite of the daily attempts pressed home by self-discipline. Yet the

---

[21] *Letters of John Marin*, letter to Stieglitz, Stonington, Maine, September 12, 1923.

outside world thought he had reached a new peak in that year. Guy Eglinton, a sensitive English youth whose instinct for painting would surely have given him a high place, had he lived, in the annals of criticism, noted that Marin's pictures began at this time to have more interior breathing space than they formerly had: they contained fewer vertical lines and more horizontals.

How to say something new? Eglinton pondered. To compare Marin to Shelley, Debussy, and the Imagist poets, was to speak truly, but also in obvious language. What to say in fresh words of a man who could make one brilliant tone play the part of twenty tones: a tone of red "that bites into the brain and poisons sleep: a green that bathes and calms the eye and spirit." Above all, Eglinton saw that Marin's faculty of "thinking in sentences and then completing them" made the work of many another painter look incomplete. [22]

Guy Eglinton was by no means alone in singing the praises of the Stonington paintings. Virgil Barker, reviewing the next Marin exhibition (February, 1924) at the Montross Fifth Avenue gallery, spoke of their "pulsating balance" in an equilibrium "at once so nearly lost and so excitingly retained." (Eglinton had created a memorable phrase, "strong impermanence," to describe the behavior of Marin's trembling forms.) Barker challenged the classification of Marin as an abstract painter. His method, he said, was a realist's method: not through imitation of the surface of nature, but through the realization of the "geometrical volumes" which characterize the quietest landscape when the eye of reality takes it thoroughly in.[23]

Along with forty-six Stonington washes of 1923 (Plates 16, 17, A), Montross showed five Palisades pictures, the work of the autumn and the following winter. In those paintings the paper was, for a change, fully covered, in the conventional Turner manner. Thomas Craven, writing of them in *The Nation*, thought they represented Marin's natural bent.[24] Thus examples of both of the two major divisions of Marin's style, the dramatic and lyrical, had their advocates.[25]

In the summer of 1924 Marin painted a small series of views of the vil-

---

[22] "John Marin, Colorist and Painter of Sea Moods," *Arts and Decoration* (August, 1924), leading article, p. 13.

[23] "The Water Colors of John Marin," *The Arts* (February, 1924), pp. 65 ff. (Reprinted, in extract, in *Art and Understanding*, Vol. I, No. 1, November, 1929, pp. 106 f.)

[24] March 19, 1924, p. 321.

[25] Up to this time (1924), no Marin had found a permanent place in any museum. Of the thirteen water colors in the Philip L. Goodwin Collection, which was now inaugurated with the purchase, at a higher price than ever theretofore paid, of *Schooner Yacht Coming*, Stonington, 1923, two were ultimately presented to museum collections: *Maine Island, from Deer Isle* to the Yale Art Gallery, and *Waves and Buoy, Maine* to the Museum of Modern Art in New York. *Blue Sea, Crotch Island*, shown at Montross, ultimately went to the Addison Gallery of American Art at the Phillips Academy, Andover, Massachusetts.

lage of Stonington, looking up from the harbor, and another from the hillside town looking out over the ocean towards Isle au Haut, some eight miles out to sea (Plate 18). After that, on the way back to New Jersey, he stopped off to make a few water colors in the Franconia Range in New Hampshire and at Bennington, in the state of Vermont. Yet he was a sick man that year. Probably fewer than twenty paintings are assignable to 1924. And the sickness pursued him into the winter that followed.

Some time after Alfred Stieglitz's death in 1946, I spent a few days with Marin in the Cliffside studio, poring over a mass of uncatalogued work, much of it unsigned and undated. Arranging it in chronological order, we accounted for every year from 1910 to the present, except the year 1925.

"Let's see," Marin said. "That must have been the year I was sick. Look in that box over there. Those pictures have never been shown at the Place." The box contained a sizeable sheaf of fine local studies, not unlike the known work of Plate 19.[26]

Down in weight to 115 pounds from a normal 130, and suffering severe stomach pains, Marin thought he had cancer. A physical check-up showed that what he needed was medical treatment, diet, and rest. He decided to take the next few months off, with the prospect of loafing at home between daily treatments. Yet it proved possible to "scoot around locally" and make some new studies of his native terrain from the tonneau of an open automobile. By the middle of September, after making four week-end visits to his cousins, the Misses Lyda and Retta Currey, who were summering up in the Berkshires, he was able to report that he had had neither treatment nor pain for three weeks. It was "a joy to be alive," even though he lived on prunes and cracked wheat. On one of those trips to visit the cousins, he paused to paint six water colors, three at Haverstraw, some twelve miles south of Peekskill, and three at Bear Mountain. One of those pictures, called *Back of Bear Mountain,* was to create a minor sensation in the following year.

He also thought, he told Stieglitz, of trying oil paint. "Well," he wrote, "there happened to be a tube of white oil paint meandering about my joint. It came in contact with a coat of mine. It left its smear. I got some benzine and went to work and in the words of the immortal Ring Lardner, you know me Al. I don't like to work so I am afraid I shall have to give up the idea of oil painting." [27]

---

[26] The Marin archive at the American Art Research Council accounts for twenty-three additional paintings from 1925.

[27] *Letters of John Marin,* letter to Stieglitz, Cliffside, New Jersey, October 18, 1925.

E.   A Street Seeing, 1928 (water color)

The Sea and the Desert

Winter, 1925—1932

ON DECEMBER 7, 1925, ALFRED STIEGLITZ OPENED HIS NEW Intimate Gallery, a twelve-by-twenty-foot room on the third floor of the Anderson Galleries, at Park Avenue and Fifty-ninth Street, with a group of John Marin's pictures. Dedicating that narrow refuge to seven Americans whose work he proposed to show in "evolving patterns"—Marin, Hartley, Charles Demuth,[1] Arthur G. Dove, Paul Strand, Georgia O'Keeffe, and Stieglitz himself—he printed a leaflet describing his own function as follows: "The Intimate Gallery is a Direct Point of Contact between Public and Artist. It is the Artists' room. It is a Room with but One Standard. Alfred Stieglitz has volunteered his services and is its directing Spirit. . . . Every picture is clearly marked with its price. No effort will be made to sell anything to anyone. Rent is the only overhead charge." And then, in italics, at bottom, this churchlike announcement: "*Hours of Silence:—Mondays, Wednesdays, Fridays, 10–12 A.M. . . .*"

Stieglitz chose well in choosing Marin to open the Intimate Gallery: for that was the year when Henry McBride issued a challenge to all the world to debate Marin's greatness.[2] The question of Marin's greatness, he said, was a question upon which the quality of a man's intelligence hinged. "It is therefore a matter of importance," he wittily said to his followers, of whom there were many, "for you to decide quickly to which division of society you belong, the lucid or the dense; for once you know, you can arrange your life accordingly, with better chances of success, such as you are. Personally, I decided long ago for myself." His answer was "yes." Marin, he felt, ranked with the great. Museum people at last were impressed: two of the 1925 Berkshire landscapes were bought for the Brooklyn Museum.

The younger of Marin's two foster mothers, Miss Lelia Currey, died in January, while the "great" show was in progress, and was buried with her parents and Miss Jenny, her sister, in the family plot in the old-fashioned

---

[1] Charles Demuth, the newcomer, then just past forty, crippled from a childhood attack of infantile paralysis and suffering horribly from the acute pains of nephritis, was painting exquisite and finished still lifes—some people thought them almost overrefined—and, in a freer style, abstractions of architectural motifs.

[2] New York *Sun*, December 12, 1925.

57

churchyard at Grove Church, New Durham. Her estate of small properties, at home and in Sayville, Long Island, the accumulation of a lifetime of earning and saving, was divided between her nephew and nieces, the Misses Lyda and Retta, daughters of Richard Currey, the Civil War marksman. The nieces, who had made their home with their aunts after the death of their father, remained for two or three years in the house which Marin had built during his architectural interlude—Miss Lyda, the elder, as housekeeper for her sister, Miss Retta, who taught school in the West New York public school system. Then they moved out to Cliffside, to a cottage whose garden adjoined Marin's property, where they have lived ever since, in daily and sisterly contact with their cousin, the painter. Marin sadly lived "in the clouds" for six months before leaving for Stonington to resume his imperative calling.[3]

The family spent the first week of July, 1926, on the road from Cliffside, traveling up the Hudson and across Vermont and New Hampshire. Except for a couple of water colors taken from Mount Chocorua (one of them now at the Fogg Art Museum at Harvard), the sketches Marin made on the trip were not completely successful. "Have to work up to things," he told Stieglitz.[4] At the end of the journey, he found a comfortable house beyond the fringes of town in the woods, a quarter of a mile from the village of Stonington and fresh drinking water; but since he could be there for only two months, on account of John Jr.'s schooling—and had meanwhile to worry over three engines, car, boat, and pump—he was afraid he could accomplish but little. But by the end of a month he was had "by the nape of the neck" [5]—"I was hitting on all six cylinders then," he once told me—and the summer produced, after all, around fifty paintings. Although nearly all of the familiar Stonington motifs were dispersed, in these pictures, and rearranged in arbitrary and rhythmical patterns, the prevailing feeling tones were markedly calmer than in 1924. There was more looking inland and less, as it were, at the sea. There were quiet green pastures, and gentle fall showers, and wine-colored flowers. It was one of Marin's peak years.

The excitement carried over into the autumn and winter months in New Jersey. Marin complained that landscape painting at home was becoming more and more difficult, what with real estate subdivisions, in the blooming twenties, "improving" the countryside to the detriment of its flora. (He was inflated by the Florida bubble himself and gave the value of two or three

[3] *Letters of John Marin*, letter to Stieglitz, Cliffside, New Jersey, June 10, 1926.

[4] *Letters of John Marin*, letter to Stieglitz, Stonington, Maine, July 19, 1926. (The following letter, from Chocorua, New Hampshire, is incorrectly dated August 7, 1926. It was written July 7, 1926.)

[5] *Letters of John Marin*, letter to Stieglitz, Stonington, Maine, September 11, 1926.

pictures for an immaterial piece of St. Petersburg property.) He went back to Manhattan to "play around" with the city streets, producing the "Movements" described as *Related to Downtown New York* (Plate B).

It might be said, on the whole, that the paintings of 1924 to 1926 reached Marin's farthest limit in the abstract process—until, in 1946, he began quite frankly and consciously to think first of paint and then of subject matter. But even during the years when he carried the process so far, he never quite let go of his motif's identity. When the wholeness of an individual subject was sacrificed to enhance the total significance—as, say, a house might be lost in an impression of "village"—color restored the individual meaning (Plate C). When Lewis Mumford saw the pictures on exhibition at the Intimate Gallery in the month of November, he thought the recent work was "among the finest fruits of our generation." It kept the surface charm of the lyrical paintings, he thought, and reached new depths of spiritual feeling. . . .[6]

An untitled pamphlet published by Stieglitz on April 17, 1927, so authoritatively describes its author's method of handling Marin's affairs at the period now under discussion that it seems to require more than cursory treatment.[7] It appears that Duncan Phillips, director and founder of the Phillips Memorial Gallery in Washington, bought two Marin water colors at the Intimate Gallery in November, 1926: *Maine Islands,* painted in 1922 from the heights back of Stonington village, and *Gray Sea,* a severe monochrome, all sea and no sky, painted on Deer Isle in 1924, both reproduced in his book, *A Collection in the Making.* Then in December, he went to the gallery to look at *Back of Bear Mountain,* a painting that Henry McBride had written about in the New York *Sun:* one of the six water colors made in 1925 on a trip to the Berkshires. Now it happened that Stieglitz himself used to examine the verdicts of Henry McBride, sometimes adding to his own large collection of Marins (and frequently gauging gallery prices) on the basis of those *obiter dicta.* So that, as Stieglitz printed the story, he was already prepared to name a high price for *Back of Bear Mountain* if a buyer appeared.

The price which Stieglitz attached to the painting was a sum to be mentioned in whispers: it was $6,000. Mr. Phillips, so the story goes, retired to ponder it. The next day, as Stieglitz reported the incident, the collector chose two humbler items from the Bear Mountain sheaf, together with another small picture that had taken his fancy, agreeing on the price, for three pieces, of $5,000.

Still according to Stieglitz's story, about which there was much specula-

---

[6] *New Republic* (December 15, 1926), p. 112.
[7] A copy of this document may be seen in the Marin files in the art department of the New York Public Library.

tion in art-dealing circles, Mr. Phillips after all bought *Back of Bear Mountain* for $6,000. Whereupon Stieglitz made a "present," on Marin's behalf, of one of the three earlier choices, while the collector took the others for $2,610: arithmetic proving, without too much trouble, that in the end he had got *Back of Bear Mountain* for $3,610. But when Stieglitz gave it out to reporters that the phenomenal price of $6,000 had been paid for one water color, the art world was shaken. Likewise Mr. Phillips, who promptly protested. Stieglitz was disappointed and hurt. "I told Mr. Phillips," he wrote in the pamphlet which he handed out to inquirers, "that I thought he had finally gotten a glimpse of the spirit of Room 303. . . ." [8]

Somewhat sparing, in the usual way, of speaking in praise of his fellow artists, Marin had written that year a warm tribute to his friend Ernest Haskell, the distinguished etcher who had come to his death in an accident in 1925. For the catalogue of a memorial exhibition of the work of a man who "always aimed high"—it was held at the Macbeth Gallery, November 9–22, 1926, simultaneously with Marin's show at the Intimate Gallery—Marin wrote that Haskell was a master who "knew his medium and whose medium knew him so that medium and man were welded together." His description of Haskell is an important addition to a full portrait of Marin, for it describes his ideal artist. "You're not to approach the work of a man like this lightly," he said, "for he didn't feel lightly. You're not to approach this work with disrespect—for he respected his work. You're not to approach it unlovingly—for he loved his work." [9]

Marin regarded the next year, 1927, as a year of experimentation. With 1919, the first year at Stonington, it remained in his mind as a "crazy" period.[10] He found himself "constantly juggling with things, playing one thing against another," and the effect, he had to admit, often looked crazy. If he had been painting automatically, he reported, he could have said, "Good! I *am* crazy," and let it go at that. But he was painting with "deliberate, mulish willfulness" in an effort to nail down the visions which grew ever more complicated. Now the visions—"incomplete visions"—were full of "dream houses of a purity of whiteness, of loveliness of proportion, of a sparingness of sensitive detail, rising up out of the greenest of grass sward": the houses, in real life, of Wiscasset and Thomaston, Maine. The key to the paintings that year is the "sparingness of sensitive detail." Nothing useless must appear in the pictures, not an idle stroke, not a meaningless detail. Only the purest paint-

---

[8] The Marin Collection at the Phillips Memorial Gallery contains sixteen water colors, five oil paintings, and two drawings, dating from 1905 to 1945.

[9] *Letters of John Marin*, between the unpaged letters of October 8, 1926, and July 9, 1927.

[10] *Letters of John Marin*, letter to Stieglitz, Stonington, Maine, August 21, 1927.

ing, only the intensest emotion was to be distilled from the liquid paints (Plates 20, 21).

Stieglitz printed Marin's letter of August 21, 1927, in a mimeographed catalogue for the November, 1927, exhibition at the Intimate Gallery so that people "should have a chance at a glimpse of the real Marin through one of his letters." Perhaps a small part of it will serve the same purpose here.

> . . . . *So I've got to spoil more paper. I don't know anybody who loves their visions more than I do. But not to absolutely get them down, that's what makes me speak of spoiling paper.*
>
> *As I drive a good deal I am conscious of the road, the wonderful everlasting road, a leading onward, a dipping, a rising, a leading up over the hill to the sea beyond. To nail that, to express that, to find the means to clutch, so that there it is, that's what torments me, to show with startling conviction.*
>
> *So I make the attempt.*
>
> *Others may make and get but don't you see, it isn't my road, it isn't my over to the sea.*
>
> *And here it is. There are moments when I am unbelievably in love with myself.*
>
> *But, there are moments when I unbelievably hate myself, for being myself.*
>
> *Curiously twisted creature.*
>
> *Prejudiced as Hell.*
>
> *Unprejudiced as Hell.*
>
> *Narrow—as they make 'em.*
>
> *Broad minded next minute.*
>
> *Hating everything foreign, to a degree, with the opposite coming in, time and time.*
>
> *A shouting spread-eagled American.*
>
> *A drooping wet winged sort of a nameless fowl the next.*
>
> *But, take it easy, whoa there, pull up. . . .*

A stopover in the White Mountains on the motor trip back to Cliffside in the autumn of 1927 was more fruitful than the visit of 1926 (Plate 22). Attacking the countryside at the end and not at the start of a season of painting, the painter was able to nail it down, as he said, right away. It was cold in the mountains in October that year and his fingers moved fast. It was like old times to paint on a good frosty day: except that the water colors iced up more quickly than oils. Mountains lowered, wet lakes sparkled as the washes flowed from his brush. One of the best of the group—it was called *Echo Lake*

—found its way (as so often happened) into the Stieglitz Collection. *Presidential Range,* another superior example, went eventually to the Fogg Art Museum in Cambridge and *Franconia Range, Mountain Peaks* to the Metropolitan, along with *Pertaining to Deer Isle, The Harbor.*

Returning to Stonington for the summer of 1928, after a rather unsatisfactory attempt at tempera painting during the winter, Marin wrote an autobiographical piece to be published in *Creative Art,*[11] along with a text by Louis Kalonyme, who had just come back from a year in Europe and was struck by the "Promethean" quality of Marin's art. Seven reproductions provided a display of his work, while a biographical note listed collections in which Marin's paintings were then to be found. In addition to the Howald, Phillips, Goodwin, Meyer, and Stieglitz purchases, there were, by 1928, representations at the Metropolitan Museum of Art, the Brooklyn Museum, and Albert E. Gallatin's Gallery of Living Art on Washington Square; and in the private collections of Paul and William Haviland, Edsel Ford, Gaston Lachaise, who had recently cast Marin's portrait in bronze,[12] and Paul Rosenfeld, who by now had four or five paintings which Hart Crane, the poet, took to be comments on eternity. (Marin wrote in the catalogue of the November, 1928, exhibition, that his "greatest collection, the Dark Room Collection," was in the Lincoln storage warehouse; only "some few," he said, were "scattered about.")

In his own prose essay, as amusing and buoyant as a piece of music by Hindemith—and as hard to follow—Marin set down more of his aesthetic theory than can elsewhere be found in one place. I venture a paraphrase:

(1) The artist begins (as Marin has said before) with a flat working surface which he may not bend out of its individual flatness.

(2) He has it in mind to make a whole picture, but the whole, as in mathematics, is the sum of its parts. The parts, in Marin's view, ought to be mobile, ought to look interchangeable, except for the "focusing points," which may be nailed down in a frame of paint. The moving parts may be allowed to appear to collide, for there is always a fight going on where things are alive; yet equilibrium must be established to keep the clash of motifs under control, to save the whole from collapsing. To form the parts into a whole, the artist provides them with "lines of connection." Yet if the parts remain properly mobile, the whole picture will move; hence it is bound to the paper, lest it leave its boundaries. (The painter may not leave to the framer the job of keeping the painting within its own space.)

---

[11] October, 1928. Reprinted in *Letters of John Marin,* near the end of the unpaged volume.

[12] The Lachaise portrait, from the collection of the Museum of Modern Art, New York, is reproduced in *John Marin,* Museum of Modern Art Catalogue, opposite p. 9.

(3) Thinking again in terms of music, Marin writes of "all sorts" of rhythms; rhythms in beats, say, of one–two–three, two–two–three, three–one–one. These beats are seen and expressed in color: for color is life, the sun of life reveals all things in the colors of light.

(4) The artist must from time to time renew his acquaintance with the elemental big forms which "have everything": sky, sea, mountain, plain, and the "things pertaining thereto." If he paints with love, he will also lovingly observe the little things pertaining to the big ones—the "relatively little things that grow on the mountain's back, which if you don't recognize, you don't recognize the mountain."

Marin had never more clearly recorded his visions in accordance with theory than at Stonington this particular summer. In the month of July, in spite of a recurrence of his nagging illness, he "knocked out a few homers" (Plates 23, 24). Whatever people might say, he announced, he had produced something with quality, the pure quality he had reached for during those years of torment. He was thankful that he had found Stonington, the place which had brought him fulfillment. "I would be home, at home, in this place, these places my homes, all together my home," he told Stieglitz.[13]

The Marins paid a short visit to Small Point in August, stopping en route at Georgetown to see Gaston Lachaise, Marsden Hartley, and the Paul Strands. They stayed once more at the Alliquippa House, now thronging with spinsters, "precious virgins ranging from fifty to sixty," militant New Englanders all, descendants of stake burners—"born with ramrods for backbones," Marin said. Much depressed, he went fishing. But he also produced six paintings of Morse Mountain, a two-hundred-foot hill rising over the marshes behind the village of Small Point (Plate D).[14]

Stieglitz, recuperating from a spell of ill health at his Victorian home on Lake George in the fall of that year, invited the Marins to pay him a visit on their way back to Cliffside. Marin stopped long enough to make a new sheaf of lyrical pictures which had little relation to the Stonington fantasies. In New York, however, he seems to have returned to the Stonington mood, for *Midtown, New York* (Plate 25) handles a metropolitan theme in the manner of *Boat Fantasy* (Plate 24): the tall building in the former surrounded, like the ship in the latter, by a formal and arbitrary arrangement of objects. But then the "stir of things" in New York took hold of his fancy and feeling and he produced some strident and deeply felt paintings, like *Street Crossing, New York* (Plate 26), which conveys the confusion of a subway entrance. He

---

13 *Letters of John Marin*, letter to Stieglitz, Stonington, Maine, August 2, 1928.
14 *On Morse Mountain, No. 5* from the Goodwin Collection was published in aquatone in Edward Alden Jewell's *Americans* (New York, 1930).

was caught by the fantastic appearance of the theater district and painted a number of street scenes like *Broadway, Night,* 1929 (Plate 27), with the curiously formalized signature to go with the formal pattern of posters and lighted signs.

Stieglitz reported "record-breaking" sales from the year-end exhibition of the paintings of 1927 and 1928 at the Intimate Gallery: although St. John Ervine, the playwright and novelist, over from Ireland to lecture Americans, took the trouble, to Stieglitz's horror, to say out loud in Stieglitz's office that he disliked the pictures.[15] This was the second time in a year that Stieglitz's judgment was publicly challenged. Waldo Frank had complained in the spring that Marin was a transcendental escapist: or why, he inquired, didn't he put people into his landscapes? [16] Stieglitz encouraged Paul Strand to talk back to Frank,[17] but history does not record what he himself said to Ervine. Perhaps he was consoled when a man who belonged to the art world, a visitor but not an "outsider," announced that after six weeks of touring the U. S. A., he had found in Marin just what he was looking for.

Julius Meier-Graefe, of the *Neue Rundschau* of Berlin, was looking, it seemed, for American painting. Marin, he thought, was producing it, and, as a foreigner, he was inclined to believe that Marin alone was painting recognizably American pictures. He was delighted, moreover, to find that Marin's aesthetic sensibility left something for the outside eye to work on. Looking at the pictures attentively was to assist in the painting; spectatorship was a creative experience. One learned the symbols—as one had been taught to do by the impressionists—and then read what they were meant to convey.[18]

It was an exciting winter, perhaps too exciting, for in the spring of 1929, when Marin made plans, at the instigation of Mrs. Mabel Dodge Luhan, Mrs. Paul Strand, and Miss Georgia O'Keeffe, to visit New Mexico to see the shapes of Southwestern mountain and plain, he explained that he had felt the world was closing in on him. He was tired of "living in herds," of swimming in a "common pool." He found it hard to "keep the spirit unsoiled" in the pool, he told Stieglitz.[19] He thought the Southwest would make a nice change.

Mrs. Luhan, whom Henry McBride used to call "the modern priestess of candor," invited him to spend the month of June in her meandering house in Taos, where "curious guests" roamed around during their hostess's

[15] Henry McBride, "Modern Art," *Dial* (February, 1929), pp. 174-6.
[16] "The Re-Discovery of America, XII," *New Republic* (May 9, 1928), p. 346.
[17] *New Republic* (July 25, 1928), p. 254.
[18] "A Few Conclusions on American Art," *Vanity Fair* (November, 1928), p. 83.
[19] *Letters of John Marin,* letter to Stieglitz, Stonington, Maine, August 2, 1928.

absence. He made the acquaintance of Tony Luhan, who wore bracelets and braids and sported a clean white shirt every day when he came out from the pueblo to visit Mrs. Luhan's establishment. Then Mrs. Marin and John joined the painter for the rest of the summer in a small adobe house on the place.

Marin rolled up his sleeves and started to work, learning how to look at the countryside as he went along. He liked the jagged forms of the mountains; was struck most of all by the vastness of space in that lofty region and by the washed clarity of the atmosphere after the showers which occurred almost daily during the rainy season in summer (Plate F). He set out to paint space, unbounded space, and produced pictures sharply different from the crowded houses and boats in the Stonington papers. Accordingly, few of the New Mexican paintings used interior frames. Where these exist, they are even and pale, in contrast to the deep blue, black and broken lines of the Stonington pictures. The symbols for sky were of great use in the desert: Marin was able to avoid the banality of the cloudless afternoon sky by indicating its presence with unobtrusive patches of color (Plate 28), though he extracted all the drama from storm clouds (Plates 29, 30).

During two summers at Taos, June to October, 1929, and mid-June to mid-September, 1930, Marin made nearly one hundred water colors. Not all of them were on the grand, spacious scale. There were studies of the "little things" on the high desert floor and in green faraway canyons: sunflowers, trees, the eighteenth-century mission at Ranchos on the Santa Fe road. There were notes and pictures of San Domingo and Pueblo Indian riders and dancers and rabbit hunts (Plate 31). Seeing pieces of jewelry made out of Mexican coins by the Southwestern Indians, Marin was enchanted with their symbolic expression of natural forms. He paid close attention to the native life and felt at home in it. Joining the artists' colony in getting up an auction to pay for repairs to the pueblo of Taos, after a torrent had dug up the streets and strewn them with garbage, he painted a poster of Babe Ruth batting one of the cans with which the town had been littered.

He showed his pictures to the resident painters on Sunday mornings: to J. Ward Lockwood, for instance, a Kansan who had studied in Paris; to Andrew Dasburg, who had reversed the usual process by coming from Paris to study with Robert Henri in New York (Dasburg and Marin went fishing together); and Loren Mozley, a sensitive painter who later wrote with appreciation of Marin. This was about all the showing that many of the New Mexican series ever got before the Museum of Modern Art's Exhibition in 1936, as a matter of fact. Marin admitted that the pictures looked

65

"kind of funny," back home in Cliffside, but a letter to Paul Strand, by now his greatest crony at billiards, shows that he was sorry the people at home showed so little interest. . . .[20]

In the winter of 1929, Stieglitz opened An American Place, a gallery with two day-lighted, gray-walled exhibition rooms on the seventeenth floor of 509 Madison Avenue. With their uncovered gray cement floors and bare windows, the rooms were as "bare, economical, and severe as fireproof hospital rooms." [21] These uniquely austere quarters, in which the pictures and Stieglitz provided the warmth and vivacity, continued for three seasons to show the work of all of the painters in the group at the Intimate Gallery: Marin, Hartley, Demuth, Dove, and O'Keeffe. The Marin show with which Stieglitz opened "The Place," as it came to be called, brought in thousands of people, according to official announcement.

While the first exhibition at An American Place was still drawing its "thousands," the Museum of Modern Art opened the second full-dress show in its history, entitled "Paintings by Nineteen Living Americans." Marin was represented by six water colors: *Maine Islands,* 1922, and *Back of Bear Mountain,* 1925, from the Phillips Collection; *Red Lightning,* 1922, from the Howald Collection; *Sailboat,* 1926; *Presidential Range,* 1927, from the Fogg Museum; *Franconia Notch, Echo Lake,* 1927, from An American Place. And along with Dove and O'Keeffe, he appeared as one of eleven contemporaries in *Modern American Painters,* a handsomely illustrated volume prepared by Samuel M. Kootz that same year. Marin's place in the world was receiving acknowledgment. He was almost sixty years old.

If the East looked "screened in" when Marin began to paint it again, after New Mexico, his familiarity with the old subject matter left him free to resume the postponed development of his personal style. The paintings at Taos, for the most part, were—granting Marin's own idiom—straightforward transcripts of unfamiliar terrain. With the return to Small Point, where he spent part of the summer of 1931 and the whole summer season of 1932, he renewed the studies which had already been leading to a more pictorial emphasis on the arrangement of planes—the most crabbed and difficult element, as we shall presently see, in the Marin process (Plates 32, 33). He also went back to the use of oil color.

The family plans for 1931 called for a motor trip to Cape Cod and

---

[20] *Letters of John Marin,* letter to Paul Strand, Cliffside, New Jersey, September 20, 1930.

[21] Paul Rosenfeld, "The Marin Show," *New Republic* (February 26, 1930), pp. 48-50. Cf. Dorothy Norman, "An American Place," and Dorothy Brett, "The Room," in *America and Alfred Stieglitz* (New York, 1934), pp. 126-151 and p. 260, for fuller (if somewhat extravagant) accounts of Room 1710.

G.   *Phippsburg, Maine, 1932 (water color)*

thence to Small Point; a month at the Point; and after that, a few weeks in a shack on the Vermont shore of Lake Champlain near the Canadian border.[22] The trip to Cape Cod was not realized. In July, the Marins drove straight to Small Point, where, toward the end of the visit, Marin painted a bleak canvas of rocky coast, sea, and sky (Plate 34), as though to illustrate a pictorial doctrine he had lately formulated for Stieglitz: "Water you paint the way water is and moves— Rocks and soil you paint the way they were worked for their formation— Trees you paint the way trees grow." [23] There were times, he discovered, when in order to paint in this manner, you had to use oil pigments. Then "your paint builds itself up, molds itself, piles itself up," until it approaches the "set of things" as the rock itself does. "Lusty" was the word that came to his lips as he piled on the paint, and "lusty" proved to be a good word for such a painting as *Boats and Sea,* 1931, an oil with a rich palette of blues, browns, reds, and greens.[24]

Some of Marin's letters to Stieglitz and other good friends were published that summer—privately printed for An American Place, with an Introduction by Herbert J. Seligmann. Gerald Sykes, in reviewing the book, raised the question whether Marin's work, so difficult for so many, belonged, as some might think, to the category of olives and artichokes or to that of meat and potatoes. For himself, Sykes was persuaded that because of its simple and "savage" quality, it partook of the character of an American plate of potatoes and meat.[25]

Marin's landlord at Lake Champlain, a man with "a sort of Emersonian cast of countenance," dropped in to call with the Sunday newspaper containing Sykes's review, and Marin could see that he had gone up a "couple of pegs" in the landlord's estimation. Having had so little contact with people in his professional character, he felt very good about that small episode. When he wrote of it afterwards, he spoke not at all of the text, which had been so extremely respectful, but only of the impression it had made on his landlord and on the extraordinary assortment of boarders who thereupon began to troop after him.[26] But the painter, as painter, must have proved a great disappointment. He only went fishing.

An autumn exhibition that year inspired a deeply felt comment by Ralph Flint in *Art News:* "I no longer have any compunctions about stating my findings about Marin. I simply set down my discoveries as they come

---

[22] Unpublished letter to Stieglitz, Cliffside, New Jersey, June 28, 1931.
[23] Unpublished letter to Stieglitz, Small Point, Maine, July 20, 1931.
[24] Reproduced in *Vogue* (August 1, 1936), p. 46.
[25] New York *Herald Tribune* (August 16, 1931), book section.
[26] Unpublished letter to Alfred Stieglitz, Vermont, August 28, 1931.

and have done so many years past. These always amount to the same general totality—that he is a master way beyond his time—possessing an almost scriptural solemnity and grandeur in his pictorial approach to the world about him, having a certain sumptuousness of outlook that is akin to that of the great Old Testament writers." [27]

Paul Rosenfeld wrote in *The Nation* [28] that 1931 had been Marin's year. He saw in the letters of "the least cerebral of artists, and the most self-assured," something of "the likeness of a good little power boat, meeting the changing winds and seas of the world, and adjusting [itself] to them without loss of direction or of impetus." In a line suggestive of Eglinton's phrase, "strong impermanence," Rosenfeld spoke of Marin's pictorial balance as "incessantly displacing itself." Best of all, he examined Marin's largely uncommented textures, from shaggy to satin-smooth areas; "from tactile realizations of roundness to tactile realizations of flatness; from ethereal veil-like substance to wash possessing a stone-like consistency and weight."

By 1932, Marin was keyed up to paint monumentally. The daily chores, it was true, were demanding, because the hotel at Small Point was not open that season: "Old Mistress Maine, she makes you to lug-lug-lug. She makes you to pull-pull-pull. She makes you to haul-haul-haul." [29] But Downeastern nature was lovely, was smiling, was beautiful, with an "unforgettable love-liness, an unforgettable beauty." In that mood, one painted her with the transparent colors. Yet she also had a disconcerting way, on that rocky coast, of turning mighty and masculine; of showing tremendous shoulders braced against the sea, her "furious brother." When she showed herself in those powerful moments, a man needed oil paint to describe her.

Marin made eight large, sweeping seascapes with "piled up" impasto areas majestically conveying that observable and inevitable "set of things" of which he had written to Stieglitz. Grandly conceived, executed with heroic, two-handed strokes of the brush, they now dazzle the eye with a brilliantly jeweled palette of light red, ultramarine, cerulean, and vert emer-aude. Painted out of doors, on the beach, the impact of their close approach to ocean is prodigious: as though one were Endymion, "the giant sea above his head." And if the spectator truly feels at the point of engulfment, he has understood the artist's intention; for here, if ever, Marin has mystically entered into his subject matter and drawn the spectator in with him. A less

---

[27] *Art News* (October 17, 1931), p. 3. Cf. the same writer's understanding account of the New Mexican water colors in *Art News* (November 8, 1930).

[28] January 27, 1932, pp. 122-124.

[29] Unpublished letter to Stieglitz, Small Point, Maine, August 28, 1932.

mystical, more realistic note was struck in the oil paintings made in the fall in home territory, as instanced in *Old Dutch Home,* painted at Tappan, New York, on the Jersey line above Norwood.[30]

Yet the new paintings were not generally well received by the public the following autumn. They confused people who had only recently come to see, with Marsden Hartley, that their author was a great handler of the water-color techniques. Lacking the grace and the elegance of the transparent papers, they stunned most of Marin's admirers—excepting faithful Henry McBride, who wrote that although the painter, "weighted down with the heavier ballast of the earthy ochres," did not fly so high as in the water colors, he got off the ground. And flight, he assumed, was "all that a citizen of the earth asks of an artist." [31] (For myself, seeing them again only lately, I should be hindsightedly tempted to choose the 1932 oil paintings above all else to that date. The wit, dash, and grace of the superb 1927–1928 Stonington papers may not be in their nature, but brilliance, monumentality, and deep emotion are abundantly there.)

The distinguished water colors of the same year were painted on excursions along the Maine coast from Popham Beach, at the mouth of the Kennebec, to Mount Desert Island and Frenchman Bay. One of the most delightful of that season's series—perhaps because the virtuosity in the handling of planes does not dim the spectator's recognitory enjoyment—is the water color called *Phippsburg, Maine* from the Stieglitz Collection (Plate G). The two versions of *Deep-sea Trawlers* (Plate 35) are memorable for showing the last sailing fleet Marin ever painted from life. He looked out on the harbor one morning to see it filled with a fleet of Portuguese trawlers and hurried down to the shore to nail them to paper. Since that time, he has painted most of his sailboats from memory.

---

[30] Reproduced in color in *Fortune* (December, 1935).
[31] New York *Sun* (November 19, 1932), unsigned. Margaret Breuning, New York *Evening Post* (November 19, 1932), thought the oils showed an "advance" over earlier years, but to her they seemed unpleasantly "painty."

The Introduction to Fame

1933—1938

VISITS TO MOUNT DESERT ISLAND IN 1932 WHETTED MARIN'S appetite for more remote segments of the weathered Maine coast. He moved on to Cape Split in Washington County, the most easterly parcel of land in the country, and there he discovered, like the diarist of the Waymouth Expedition in 1605, that he liked the Maine coast the better the farther Down East he went. In a nostalgic (and unpublished) letter written from Cliffside to one of his Downeastern friends some years later, he said that Cape Split lay nearer his heart than any place in the world.

For his first summer there, in 1933, he took an old-maidish, whatnot-filled house known as the Godfrey cottage, just inside the Cape on the road out from Addison. His new neighbors, the Wasses and Tabbutts, the Crowleys and Plummers—descendants of British colonists who had moved eastward from Martha's Vineyard, around 1765, to fish cod in Wescogus River—lived off the land and the sea, and Marin, following his own instincts, fed his family from the same natural sources. "We eat fish morning, noon, and night," he told Stieglitz.[1]

He looked round about him all the more sharply because he quickly discovered that the "fisher folk" of the place knew the Cape rock by rock, reef by reef, tree by tree. He wanted not to "play fiddlesticks with their particular chest of drawers," he told Stieglitz, and was pleased to report that he could "still see across the road without glasses." [2] The change from Small Point, though delightful, was not revolutionary. Marin was therefore able to "play around" with his motifs almost at once, producing "quite a batch" of new paintings that passed his own critical muster (Plates 36, 37, 38).[3]

The autumn showing at An American Place in that year, called "Twenty-five Years of Marin," was a retrospect beginning with the Seine water colors, which showed him, by comparison with their stormy successors, to have been a "carefree young man singing in the fields through mere excess

---

[1] Unpublished letter, Addison, Maine, July 19, 1934.

[2] Unpublished letter to Stieglitz, Addison, Maine, July 30, 1933.

[3] An oil painting made in the winter of 1933, *Fifth Avenue Looking West at Forty-second Street* was exhibited in 1940 at the Carnegie (Pittsburgh) "Survey of 160 Years of U. S. Painting," and was reproduced in *Art News*, October 26, 1940, p. 16.

70

of energy." [4] Then, after taking "a little naughty pleasure" in being hiero-glyphic, he had turned, the pictures seemed to say, to drama—achieving the "loftiness of style that arrives when an artist successfully copes with tragedy." An extraordinary thing that nobody had as yet troubled to notice was that McBride's recapitulation of a quarter century of Marin's history traced a cycle that can be reconstituted about every eighteenth month from 1912. That Marin has been all things at all times, so to speak, is the mark—as compared to the "period" painters—of his perfect consistency.

Returning to Cape Split in 1934 on a last-minute impulse (as he now re-calls it), the artist bought the house upon Pleasant Bay where he still spends the summer. Built in the mid-nineteenth century by one of the Longfellows to house summer boarders—although the Longfellows really belonged to the near-by town of Machias—it contained an ancient Chickering concert grand piano of weathered appearance and exceptional tone. Marin counted 281 panes of glass on the sun porch which he proposed to use as a studio. Her-bert J. Seligmann, a Cape Split summer resident and editor of Marin's "racy and delightful" letters, reported to his Manhattan circle that the walls of the house were painted in hot-dog color trimmed with molasses.

"One of the sorrows of owning a place is that you cannot send for the *Landlord* to fix the stopped-up kitchen drain—you have to do your own fixing," Marin later wrote Stieglitz.[5] He cleaned out the fireplace chimney with a small Christmas tree, whitened the walls to make a better background for the pictures, and bought a twenty-five-foot boat with an engine which ran, that first year, as "smooth as a sewing machine."

Marin's Maine, then, these last fifteen years, has been Cape Split, Pleas-ant Bay, the numerous offshore islands which he has explored in his motor-boat, the coast between Mount Desert and Eastport, and a thirty-mile range of back country between the Tunk Mountains and Machias River. This companionable area has provided him, away from home, what he had long treasured at Cliffside; namely, an ideal pattern for his habit of work—the constant and manifold elaboration of familiar themes, the production of several versions and treatments of a particular motif in a quick series of "sittings" or over a succession of seasons.[6]

Yet in 1934 he feared that his output would not be "stupendous." There was too much to do and so much to see. But there was just an off-chance that his work might go better—"with the looking outward over the

---

[4] Henry McBride, New York *Sun* (October 28, 1933).
[5] *Twice A Year* (Spring-Summer 1939), letter to Stieglitz, Addison, Maine, August 18, 1935, p. 183.
[6] An enchanting series of twelve small oil paintings of 1939 follows the course of the spring months in a piece of hill country between Cliffside and Tuxedo Park. *See* Chapter VII.

waters, the ledges, the islands, the happenings on the waters, the being as it were placed on the sea itself—the porpoises and the loons a-playing at one's very doorstep—at first to say the least quite flabbergasting. . . ." [7] He spoke again the next year of the porpoises: "In front of us the bay and islands and smooth water and rough water and the porpoises a-chasing after herring —the house is so close to the water I almost feel at times that I am on a boat— then there are those Sun Sets—we make 'em to order—the kind *no* artist can paint. . . ." [8]

The output, whether better or worse in its quality, contained many new elements: some pink bathers on canvas (Plate 39); and some new symbols for water (Plates 40, 41). The new symbols suggesting the sea were created on the view that too much sea, now that he owned a house on it, was as tedious to behold in a painting as too much blue sky. Another device which appeared at Cape Split was the free use of remembered experience, the filling out of the present from past recollections. Lobster fishermen there hauled their traps from boats fitted with motors; hence the three-master and four-master schooners that sailed into Marin's Pleasant Bay pictures had to be called up out of memories of a day that was passing. And some of the new subject matter appeared accidentally, as when stump-tailed porcupines nibbled the bark from a row of trees on the beach overnight. Marin rushed down from his cottage next morning to paint the stripped trunks and branches.

Marin had gaily told Stieglitz that he always thought about painting with oils when the water ran low.[9] The water that year must have run low in Cliffside as well, for the next exhibition at An American Place contained eight oil paintings, two from Cape Split and six from Manhattan. The New York oils followed up the new interest in the human figure, both clothed and unclothed. In the first of a series of circus pictures, augmented from memory in 1936 at Cape Split,[10] there were performers, for instance, who had forgotten to put on their tights (Plate H). Likewise, of the eighteen water colors which were hung on the walls at the Place—the output had, after all, been at least average in number, though only the half were displayed at the time—a few had been made in the fall in Manhattan (Plate 42).

One of the offshore islands which Marin frequented in 1935 was Outer Sand Island—so called, he supposed, "because there is no sand on it—but

[7] *Twice A Year* (Spring-Summer 1939), letter to Stieglitz, Addison, Maine, August 28-30, 1934, p. 183.
[8] *Twice A Year* (Spring-Summer 1939), letter to Stieglitz, Addison, Maine, August 18, 1935, pp. 183-4.
[9] Unpublished letter to Stieglitz, Addison, Maine, July 30, 1933.
[10] Unpublished letter to Stieglitz, Addison, Maine, August 30, 1936.

great granite slabs a-piled up by those great forces thousands of years ago." Under the lee of that island, he told Stieglitz, he saw two little sea pigeons, "a-floating on the waves—and oh so beautiful—one's heart went out to them. . . . There they floated," he wrote, "the pair—with nature's caring—with the mating season once a year—the rest of the time perfectly happy and content to be near one another—no complicated depressions—when the storm approached they had their wings to take them to some sheltered place under the lee of the storm. Being a human one cannot help but think in contrast— of the human species with his chasings—his inventions—with his mix ups and trouble manufacturing and sex problems and Woman's rights—and man's rights. Now these two little sea pigeons accepted their difference and were glad—were content—wouldn't have it otherwise. There is one thing man has made that *approaches* [the life of sea pigeons]—*music—art*—and *poetry*—these three made with no other thought than to create beauty—a something that is wistful and lovable, a something that is cold as ice and of an aloofness indescribable to all that is dross and ugly—'choose ye this day whom ye shall serve.' " [11]

The intense emotion derived from that season's communion with nature was distilled into a small number of oils (about seven) which were thought by those who believed in them to be incredibly beautiful in their cold authority, their grand aloofness; and by others to be unendurably crabbed (Plate 43). Stieglitz was obliged to eke out the next exhibition (October 27-December 31, at the Place) with twelve water colors left over from the previous summer.

Marin was painting in oil again the next year. "There are a couple of oil paintings slowly drying in places—the paint is on thick," he wrote Stieglitz. "As paint costs money, the thicker the paint the more you ought to get for the picture or the thicker the paint the more wasted—therefore the more is the penalty. . . . Since the above writing I have added another oil to the collection and expect if the day comes along to add another. . . . Four Master pieces ought to be enough." [12]

He daily consulted a Dutch barometer on his writing table to keep track of the weather. Fair weather at hand, Hansel and Gretel appeared at the door, Hansel in blue and Gretel in yellow. A witch in a blue dress with brown cowl and apron prophecied stormy weather. When Hansel and Gretel showed up together, Marin collected his brushes and paints and went out.

[11] *Twice A Year* (Spring-Summer 1939), letter to Stieglitz, Addison, Maine, August 18, 1935, pp. 183-5.
[12] *Twice A Year* (Spring-Summer 1939), letter to Stieglitz, Addison, Maine, September 10, 1936, p. 185.

"For subject matter I don't go very far," he wrote. "I stick a boat in here and there from past experience of boats." And speaking of boats (the letter goes on), the writer remembered that "there was a fellow who worked very differently from the way I work and that chap was Boudin—but he knew his boats—Hartley has a profound respect for him too—he told me so. I saw a painting of a boat in I think the Metropolitan—to me it was a joke—to me Manet didn't know boats—didn't know the sea."

When I reminded Marin of this letter one morning, the witch having reported that the weather was not right for painting, Marin spoke again of Boudin. "Boudin is very much underrated," he said. "He is a fine painter. He had such an affection for boats and the beach. He put in all the lines—that's what people did in those days—but he never spoiled the essence of *boat*."

He spoke at length of the relationship of line to painting. "I hate lines drawn with a brush," he remarked. "They are not strong enough. In a water color, lines are easy. You draw your lines with a pencil. Do you know how I sometimes make lines with oil paint?"

I confessed that I didn't.

"I fill up a glass ear syringe with diluted oil paint, usually black paint, and while I press on the plunger, I draw. It's like using a pencil. You can put down a definitive line. . . ."

The oil paintings he was making in 1936 included a circus piece, done from memory (Plate 44), and a few seascapes. Since he did not return to Cape Split until the middle of August, there were not many water colors. The few that were made formed a kind of delicate counterpoint to the oil paintings. Using the pencil freely for drawing, he produced some bravura transparencies which seem to have been intended to illustrate the extreme difference inherent in the two mediums (Plate 45). The small number of sea studies was filled out with views of Manhattan put down in the winter (Plates 46, 47). That winter was a great time for Marin. . . .

He was in his sixty-sixth year when the Museum of Modern Art in New York extracted his candle from under Stieglitz's bushel and set it up where twenty thousand people could see it. This first Marin exhibition of national consequence, spaciously hung on two floors and opened to the public on October 21, 1936, was a retrospect composed of one hundred and sixty water colors, twenty-one oil paintings, and forty-four etchings, chosen by Stieglitz and borrowed from nine private collectors, four major museums, and An American Place.

Marsden Hartley remarked once again, in the catalogue, on the phenomenal accuracy of both observation and brush stroke, qualities for which

74

Chinese painters were famous in the time of Hui Tsung, when stenographic realism in color was greatly valued in China. "No one has known better what the prescribed wash can do," Hartley said, "no one has made it more powerful, more velvety, more metallic, more acrid or more sinister and more provocative of the great sources of nature. . . . No one has so completely realized in this medium the exact condition of a high moment. . . . Take in a few Turners, all so thin and pale and if perhaps slightly evocative, never having that brute arm of thought behind them. . . . You will never see water colors like these of John Marin again so take a good look and remember, and if you are a painter, don't try to cope with the style because the style in this case is several times the man, love of life, love of work, love of nature." [13]

Elizabeth Noble, in a sympathetic review of the august occasion, said that Marin had created "an almost perfect cryptogram of man's observation in reaction to nature." The pictures were not to be taken in at a glance, she correctly inferred; the "meaning" was sometimes hidden in symbols. The spectator was required to get out his intellectual glasses and polish them up; to acquaint himself with the Marin language. The same thing was true, as Miss Noble suggested, of the poems of Emily Dickinson, who, like Marin (and Thoreau) was a transcendentalist in her relation to nature. Robert Frost, simplifying a similar theme in a Cambridge lecture, drew attention to a group of his poems published as "Editorials" in the volume called *Steeple Bush*. The "Editorials" were not "pure" poetry, the poet remarked. They were "applied" poems. They had a didactic function, a social purpose. The rest of the volume, he hoped, was pure poetry. Miss Noble had seen that Marin's work was "pure" art. Hence she supposed that, in a humanistic and socializing era, it might seem to some people to be too unworldly.[14]

Marin's friend Loren Mozley, the painter from Taos, contributed a pen-portrait in the Museum of Modern Art "Bulletin" for the month of October: "John Marin is an American original, a curious little man, wiry and frail. His face is incredibly wrinkled and puckers into all sorts of criss-cross lines. His candid eyes peer out brightly and mischievously under an outlandish curling bang. . . . When he comes to town he dresses with a quaint old-fashioned elegance. A few freckles. A dark blue tie knotted in a remembered way. A pearl. And a tense grace born of habitual alertness: the axis under control. . . ."

The artist could find only one flaw in the literary proceedings. It was not generally thought that the twenty-one oils added anything to his stature. Some observers found that half were too thin, too like the water colors in

---

[13] "As to John Marin, and his ideas," *John Marin*, Museum of Modern Art Catalogue, pp. 15 ff.
[14] *Art Front* (December 18, 1936).

treatment, while others found a half all too thickly painted, too unlike the transparencies. Marin was necessarily somewhat bewildered. There was emotional comfort to be taken, however, in his hometown paper, the Union City *Hudson Dispatch,* which carried a story about how a Bergen County boy had made good.[15]

Marin was ill again much of the time in the spring and summer of the next year—with neuritis, lumbago, sciatica, and "new pains down the front of my leg." He had made some pen drawings with China ink in New York during the winter, witty and humorous sketches that expressed his rather innocent gaiety somewhat more clearly than the paintings had done. And after the first of the year, a part of the exhibition at the Museum of Modern Art had been hung in Washington, at "Studio House," the Phillips Memorial Gallery, in the second showing that Marin had ever had outside of New York: [16] the first having been a small exhibition in 1926 at the enterprising Chicago Art Institute.

August came and he could not yet promise Stieglitz enough pictures to continue the unbroken succession of one-man shows. He painted his first water color that summer on August 4. "I tell you," he wrote Stieglitz, "it felt good to get out there again with my subject matter." [17] He chose motifs that lay near his house. There were several studies, for instance, in water color and oil, of various stages in the fourteen-foot tide which flows into a small rocky cove at the foot of the path from the house to the bay side— simple and moving transcriptions of rocks, water, and sky (Plate 48). Perhaps because he had starts of illness, he was painting that year in alternations of depressed, muted color and in high-keyed bursts of bright tones of reds and purples (Plates 49, 50).[18]

Marin seemed to experience almost equally, during the autumn, the "joys and irritations" of the act of artistic creation; the irritations of failure to achieve his intention and the joys of the sensuous aspect of painting. "When I squeeze the red out of the tube and it's molded into its working surface to my molding, I have delight," he told Stieglitz. "And when I

---

[15] Editorial page, October 22, 1936.

[16] H. Parks Klumpp, of the Fine Arts Division, Library of Congress, told the readers of the Washington *Post* (February 7, 1937) that Marin's achievement had issued from the relentless pursuit of his own private course. Sibilla Skidelsky, reporting an interview with the painter at the home of his stepbrother, Charles Bittinger, wrote in a complimentary vein on his craftsmanship in the Washington *Post* (February 7, 1937).

[17] Unpublished letter to Stieglitz, Addison, Maine, August 1, 1937.

[18] Jerome Mellquist, "Marin and His Oils," *The Nation* (March 12, 1938), pp. 308 f., describes the colors of the brighter 1937 oils: "Purples burst from the sea, supported by deep blues. On the shore are sober browns and blacks. . . ." Marin was represented by that year's *Sea with Red Sky* at the Carnegie International in October, 1938.

H.   Circus Forms, 1934 (oil)

squeeze the blue out of the tube and it is molded onto its working surface to my molding, I have delight. . . . The delight of others I share in part only —I cannot fully share—as others cannot share fully my delights— These [are] my eyes that see as others cannot see. These are my ears that hear as others cannot hear." [19]

The work of that season was more austere than charming and Stieglitz remarked that it would not be easy to sell. Marin had no misgivings. It happened that a painting of birch trees on Jordan's Delight, an exposed island where such trees had no "right" to bear the brunt of tempestuous weather, was one of his "all-time favorite" pictures. Yet he promised to paint some more salable pictures in the following year.[20]

In the autumn at home, Marin painted a group of Manhattan street scenes with figures, so that there was, after all, a respectable number of new paintings for the next show, held in February, 1938, at An American Place. At the request of Stieglitz, he composed a long poem to "explain" the oil paintings to viewers:

To my Paint Children
      To you who have been in the
making—these many years—
      and who are now made to the
best of my making
      and do now find yourselves
hung in all your seeming nakedness—on these walls
      bear yourselves well and
disclose no more than can be disclosed by
your being what you are
      Hold yourselves aloof—hold
yourselves—strange—with a strange
strangeness
      Tempt those who can be tempted
and for those—cease not to tempt—but if
one says "he has you" go you into hiding

      Now—my Paint Kids—Poppa—
knows you are Splayed in parts—are weak
in parts

---

[19] Unpublished letter to Stieglitz, Cliffside, New Jersey, September 23, 1937.

[20] *Twice A Year* (Spring-Summer 1939), letter to Stieglitz, Addison, Maine, July 18, 1938, p. 189. (This is the only recorded occasion upon which Stieglitz asked Marin to keep an eye on the market: a remarkable record.)

77

John Marin

With here and there—of a part
missing—inarticulate—but not so much so
but that Poppa gets a meaning
     yes you are incomplete—you are
not quite rigged up—there'll be here and there
a—missing—to complete your balanced order
     that's where your Poppa hasn't
quite clicked—your baffled Poppa—still you
have each and every one *somewhat* clicked—some
few of you *somehow* clicked
     so that Even the most crippled of
you—well he loves you all—you're his
     love-paint-children—and
however you are looked at—don't change yourselves—just keep—being yourselves—
     you ask no questions—you
answer no questions
     you move in your own movings
Content to play in your own little yards
he—your Poppa—has surrounded you with
each a little fence—
     each fence perhaps hurriedly
made perhaps not too well made—just like
yourselves—
     your fence now becomes a part
of you—I hope it won't hinder your playing—
I trust it will serve to make you play the
harder within yourselves—knowing your
boundaries—
     and if your fence does keep
them—who would see—from seeing you too
intimately—it will make to tantalize—
so that they will be made—as it were—
to take peeps through the pickets—

     your Poppa had quite a job
in the making of you—
     We will give them quite a job
if they really want to see you
     Now there have been Somethings
said about the which I will now speak

The Introduction to Fame

you see—you my—water paint
kids and you my—Oilpaint—Kids are different
     but you were made each and every
one of you by that same old Codger—your
Poppa—
     I would say you are neither the
one or the other to be jealous of one another
     to you my Oil Kids—your Poppa—
got a somewhat reputation a making your *water*
sisters
     but you Seem to be a Coming along—
tolerably well—tolerably well—maybe a little
haltingly but still a moving I hope—as to why
I speak of this there be those who have said—
may still say—You should never have been born—
     Give them not a thought—
You are not if you are not
but you *Are* if you *are* and *that's that*
Now to all of you *again be yourselves*
     behave as individuals—
to the Extent that you have these ingredients
within you—as healthy—well balanced
individuals should behave
     Wherever you go—and Poppa
hopes that those of you who—go—wont
become lonesome—will have a warm habitation—
will be allowed to live—will be in good
Company—deserving good company and for
those of you who return back to him
     well—Poppa too knows where
a few fatted calves are to be found
     now to all of you *don't forget*
—thank warmly—the man who's made it
possible your being where you are
     So long Kids—Poppa salutes
you—again don't meddle in other people's
affairs—if they love our AFFAIR—dance to
them Kids—DANCE—your loving Poppa

         JOHN MARIN

79

In the summer of 1938, when the witch on the studio porch called more signals than Gretel, so that Marin was kept much indoors, he managed to produce one of his most weighty oil paintings, *Hurricane*, the color of which was laid on thickly, light red flecking a surface of cobalt green, a "lost" color.[21] He also made a rare still life, the oil painting *Laurel Blossoms in Vase* (Plate 51). But most of the time, when kept in by the weather, he sat on the glassed-in verandah and looked out on the sea. "It is now a green gray," he wrote in September, "and the rain clouds are a racing atop it, a spilling their showers on it—it can take it—it can take heaps and not notice it. All the writings of man about it—all the ravings of poets about it—don't bother a particle— It looks its best in broad day light when it's all revealed in all its big Saltiness— You Can Smell it afar off— When you are on it you are enveloped in its—BIG SMELL— To bring something of this back—I for one—hope . . . that my paint too shall smell—a little smell—as a minute equivalent to that great salty smell—out there—that it shall give forth an honest healthy stench that shall—a bit—counterbalance unholy vulgarity." [22]

One day he painted a seascape indoors, for the gray green of the sea was too good to lose. "I slapped a boat in there—plenty of wind—so I heeled her over— There now she moves, a painted boat in her paint sea— Her gray green paint Sea—a sea curling white about the boat—a sea curling white about the ledges—and if you put on the paint right it will find its own depth and if you paint that boat right it will tell its own story. . . . But again paint the boat right and forget the story, paint the sea right and forget the story."

In the midst of the curling sea, just under his nose, there appeared a real boat heading to Eagle Island through a half gale from the northwest. Marin abandoned the fictitious boat to paint the real boat with its crew of three men fighting their way to the island. "I have stopped everything to paint that little boat—to surround it with the sea and still keep *boat*—that's my job. . . . Well," he said, when he went back to the letter, "I've Scotched the three men in the little boat."

---

[21] This painting was sold in 1944 for $16,000.

[22] *Twice A Year* (Spring-Summer 1939), letter to Stieglitz, Cape Split, Maine, September 1, 1938, pp. 185 ff.

The Beautiful Earth

1939—Summer, 1946

THE LETTERS OF 1938–1939 SHOW MARIN FEELING AT HOME with the Cape Split lobster fishermen. "I am a small-town gink with a small-town disposition," he told Stieglitz.[1] He liked the reserved, unpretentious people amongst whom he had settled and they responded by giving him their affectionate friendship. His closest friends on the Cape, Mr. and Mrs. William Thompson—Susie and Bill to their neighbors—had spent their honeymoon, some twenty years earlier, in the Longfellow house (Marin's house) while they built their own cottage on the road to the head of the Cape. Mrs. Thompson and Mrs. Marin saw each other daily in summer, although the former was many years younger. It always seemed to Mrs. Thompson, she told me, that the friendly Marins kind of chose to be commonplace. Unlike summer folks generally, they put on no airs. Mrs. Thompson approved of the way in which Mrs. Marin kept a neat house, looked after her husband and son, and made pets of stray cats and spiders.

Mrs. Thompson, born Susie Wass, and first cousin (once removed) to Mme. Nordica, the singer who was born Lillian Norton over in Farmington, in Kennebec County, in an earlier epoch, is a woman of such great personal beauty and personal style that Marin, never a painter of portraits, has frequently asked her to sit to him and she has as often obliged. Over the years of their friendship, it has kept him busy trying to point out some hidden thing in the woods that she has missed on her daily sallies into the meadows and woods, where, like the painter, she has cultivated all the phases of nature—rejoicing in seasonal changes for their sheer, impractical beauty as well as for the fruits they yield up to her larder. Marin is as pleased as a boy to turn up a red-berried witchwood at the end of the swamp in exchange for Mrs. Thompson's unexpected discovery of a moosewood standing deep in the pine lot.

"I declare, John knows where everything is on the Cape," Bill Thompson said, when Marin came into the Thompson's cookroom one day with a cap full of huckleberries, picked from the only known bush in the township.

Mr. Harry Wass, Mrs. Thompson's father, and owner—so the neighbors

---

[1] Unpublished letter to Stieglitz, Addison, Maine, July 12, 1939.

boast—of the finest strawberry patch in the state of Maine, retired from lobster fishing about the time the gasoline contraptions came in. He fished for a living when a man thought nothing of hauling a trap from some fifteen fathoms, and had to fish winters and summers, by hand, to make the new year meet the old. In retirement, Uncle Harry, turned rural philosopher, has taken a broad view of life. When his son-in-law complained that his children raised hell, Uncle Harry Wass said, "Of course they raise hell. I raised hell when I was a boy, you raised hell, and boys and girls always raise hell. There never yet was a boy or girl to do work when they could get out of it." Uncle Harry and Marin took to each other in style.

The Marins and Thompsons, who have five sons and a daughter, used to pile into Bill Thompson's boat, after the day's lobster hauling, and go out to Flint Island or Outer Sand Island to fish and cook a fish-smother supper (fish and pork boiled in sea water in an iron kettle). Marin liked to paint on Outer Sand Island, the sandless isle with "a great granite ledge with boulders ... placed there by a race of giants fifty feet tall. . . ." [2]

Before returning to Cape Split for the summer of 1939, Marin made a series of twelve oil paintings on 12" x 16" canvas with the object of following the course of the spring, from brown and gray March to leaf-green June, in a small piece of hill country in the Ramapo Mountains, some twenty miles northwest of Cliffside. Mixing his colors on a big brush, he worked with full, loose strokes and impasto accents to convey the color, light, and atmosphere of the ascending season. These delicious little pictures express all the lighthearted gaiety of nature's rebirth. With fall and winter, as the artist began to show nature creeping back to her tomb, it happened that mankind followed after. World War II had begun. Marin, brooding over the sea at Cape Split, tried to persuade himself that the war could not be avoided. "Human beings don't change," he told Stieglitz, "no more than the earth or the sun or the universe changes." He worked at complicated oil paintings, taking it slowly.

One of the letters that summer throws light on the relation of trust between Marin and Stieglitz, then of thirty years' standing. The California Water Color Society had offered Marin a room to himself in its next exhibition and the painter had turned the invitation over to Stieglitz. "I would rely on your judgment," he said. "I have written the California Society that you have the sole say-so about my art affairs and that they *might* hear from you." [3] Like many another organization which tried, in late years, to show Marin's paintings, the California Water Color Society had to put up with

---

[2] Unpublished letter to Stieglitz, Addison, Maine, July 26, 1939.
[3] Unpublished letter to Stieglitz, Addison, Maine, August 28, 1939.

refusal.[4] Stieglitz later explained to Mrs. Dorothy Norman why he was reluctant to show Marin's work in joint exhibitions. Marin, he said, wouldn't have taken prizes in the museums.[5] Yet there was no question of prizes when Marin was offered a great one-man exhibition in Paris, and that too was rejected by Stieglitz. And when in 1946 Marin (by proxy) reached England at last, through government channels, he was hailed as America's top-ranking painter by R. H. Wilenski, English critic of highest standing.[6]

Thus leaving to Stieglitz all such matters as exhibitions and sales, Marin continued to search for motifs to engage his interest while the world was at war. Driving the rough road down Cape Split in August, 1940, he discovered a motif which involved his descent to a rocky ledge two hundred feet below the crest of the cliff which forms the Cape's head. He cut a series of footholds through a tangle of fir trees that clung to the ledge and scrambled down with his easel, two canvas stretchers, and paint box and palette. "The wind she did blow," he reported. Mosquitoes were thick when he reached the quieter rock shelf below, but he made his two paintings and hauled himself back up the cliff. Four months later, celebrating his seventieth birthday, he boasted that he could still climb a tree to scale off its branches, chop it down at the trunk, saw it into stove lengths, and split it.

One detects, in a letter of that seventieth year, an increasing intensity in the painter's devotion to painting and withal a tendency—without growing unfriendly—to withdraw ever more secretly into the innermost privacy of his Palace of Art. That Palace of Art was no Tennysonian pleasure-house, to be sure. No gilded gallery "lent broad verge" to far lands; no "long-sounding corridors" connected baronial chambers. Marin could count on only one room to himself at Cape Split, and that the front room of his cottage, with a fireplace in the northeastern corner and a porch along its southern exposure. But the view from that room, like Tennyson's,

> . . . show'd an iron coast and angry waves.
> You seem'd to hear them climb and fall
> And roar rock-thwarted under bellowing caves
> Beneath the windy wall.

---

[4] In earlier years, Marin paintings and etchings had been occasionally placed in mixed exhibitions: e.g., Buffalo (1910, 1921); Providence (1911); Philadelphia (1911, 1913, 1914, 1918, etc.); Worcester (1912, 1924); Chicago (1915, 1916, 1926, 1928, etc.); Rochester (1917, 1924); Los Angeles (1920); Syracuse (1920); Detroit (1921); Milwaukee (1921, 1929, 1930); Dallas (1922); Baltimore (1923); Florence (1927); Boston (1929); Atlantic City (1929); Cincinnati (1930, 1931, 1932); Stockholm (1930). See *The Index of Twentieth Century Artists* (October, 1933), pp. 12-16.
[5] Alfred Stieglitz, "Six Happenings," *Twice A Year* (Fall-Winter 1946–47), p. 199.
[6] "A London Look at U. S. Painting," *Art News* (August, 1946), p. 26. Cf. *Magazine of Art* (December, 1946), p. 382.

The pictures he looked at, however, as they leaned against the breast of the chimney, were his own paintings. Sitting in a wicker chair across the room from the mantelpiece, during hours of rest and unrest, he examined them with loving severity.

"Are they good?" he inquired. "Well, they are as good as they are," he replied. "You cannot take that away from them—nor can they look better than they are—you can add nothing, you can take away nothing. I demand of them that they are related to experience. I demand of them that they have the story. [I] demand [of them] that they have the music of themselves so that they do stand of themselves as beautiful—forms—lines—and paint on beautiful paper or canvas." [7]

The demand that they "have the story" does not, of course, refer to anything remotely resembling *storytelling*. The wave breaking on the shore, the wave that "makes the artist to hum": the painter's perception of "wave" is what Marin meant by the "story." If an artist made a painted wave breaking on a painted shore so that the spectator would be "made to hum," he would be telling the story in the Marin sense. He would not go on to *copy* nature's wave breaking on nature's shore. That would have been a vile presumption upon nature's beauty: for a picture is art, not nature. The wave must be paint and the shore must be paint, unmistakably. Those are the terms—I do not attempt here to define them—in which Marin was thinking. And they are the terms which chiefly fill his mind at this moment of my recording his thought. Since they are the loftiest (i.e., most abstract) terms of his aesthetic theory, more remains to be said of them in the ultimate chapter.

There was a wonderful storm during August, the kind of storm called a tempest in the Downeastern idiom. Warning signals were sent out along the Maine coast to call small craft into places of safety. When the storm broke loose, the Marins piled into their car and went to the head of the Cape to see the grand sight. "Those seas out there," Marin wrote, "could take all the inhabitants of the earth and spew them about." [8] At the next exhibition at An American Place,[9] the heaviness of the turbulent sea, expressing emotionally the weight of war on the mind, could be felt in the impasto oil paintings, once more so properly distinguished from the transparencies of the swift water colors (Plate 52).

---

[7] Unpublished letter to Stieglitz, Addison, Maine, August 31, 1940.
[8] *Ibid.*
[9] December 11, 1940–January 21, 1941. The catalogue reprinted complimentary notes by Angna Enters, who compared the individual "swing" of the water colors to the unmistakable gait of American sailors whom the dancer had seen on leave in Villefranche.

The Beautiful Earth

When National Art Week was decreed for November, 1940, under White House auspices, the Editor of *Palisadian,* a newspaper edited at Cliffside and published at Palisade, New Jersey, invited Marin, as a Cliffside Park artist, to write a guest editorial. Marin contributed the following sapient and self-explanatory paragraphs about art and nationality: [10]

To the public:

It is Said—We are becoming—Art-Conscious—therefore let there be an—Art Week—focused on work done in—of and by America.

That out of it all will blossom forth—that—worth the looking at—

This is the hope—

produce the artist and—presto—realization—not so fast—know you—that the artist is—not too Common—and that produced he must have Encouragement—though courageous himself—he must have—like others about him—a good living—to do good work—this the art conscious public must help to bring about by purchasing that which they profess to love.

For the public to know—to discern the artist—the one who is— from the one who professes to be—isn't too easy.

One says—"I live here"—"I use the objects of my locality—for subject matter"—it gets him nowhere—if he is not an Artist. For one living in Australia may be better than he of our soil.

It is a legitimate hope though that our soil will produce the artist.

The people must gradually learn to discern the fine things—those sensitive to beauty can—those not sensitive cannot.

Those sensitive will want—and if the want is great enough—the artist will appear to supply that want and—I repeat—he's to be helped —to withhold that is to disobey the law of human relationship—and rest assured that he being an artist gives as much as he gets—he gives abundantly.

This work, etc.—this artist is to be found in his—work shop—there seek him—expect him not to play the game social or of self advertisement—it would appear in his work and the sensitive ones will have none of it. Beware of the ambitious one and the one who works all the time—he hasn't time to think.

Go to him whose every effort is—the good job—

To him who delights in his living—to him who takes not himself too seriously and who can at times look and make faces at himself.

Don't rave over bad paintings.

---

[10] November 15, 1940. Quoted by permission of the Editor.

John Marin

Don't rave over good paintings.

*Don't everlastingly read messages into paintings—there's the—
Daisy—you don't rave over or read messages into it—You just look at
that bully little flower—isn't that enough!*

He broke into print again the next summer, this time as chairman of
a picture jury.[11] His "Comments on the Pictures in this Exhibition," a
pamphlet which was handed about at Princeton University during a showing of the work of New Jersey painters and sculptors, speaks of creation
versus copying:

*I can say that those picked out and maybe others pointed to a
sensitiveness which is encouraging—that they mostly showed an aware-
ness—that the picture must be a created object—that it can derive from
other created objects, but that to copy these created objects or to make
the effort to copy, places one in the position of having to defend that
which cannot be defended—for the beholder has the right to say, "I'd
rather look at the object itself than your copy."*

*There you have the artist—he being the one who puts forth that
which has its own right of existence—its own beauty.*

*One cannot create that which one sees—it's already been created
—he can create from that which he has seen.*

*The effort of the one—never the artist—to make an object as near
like the object he sees as he can.*

*The constant effort of the one—the artist—to make an object—his
picture—irrespective of any other object—he alone recognizes and has
respect for other objects.*

*The one striving after the impossible—the other striving after the
possible.*

*In the exhibition which will be placed on the walls of Princeton,
there I feel the strivings of those who seek the possible.*

Those with the possible—*art germ, a sprouting—may it, being
there, be nourished and thrive—it takes plenty of striving for—but it's
a mighty worthy strife . . . .*

The private letters of the time were full of inquiry and lamentation;
of the unrelenting conflict between art and the forces of destruction; of
the poet's theme—set in a poet's language—of immutable values in a changing world. Nature in terms of springy turf underfoot; of wild roses, daisies,

---

11 Marin served on two other juries in 1940–1941: with Charles Burchfield and Eliot O'Hara, in
judging a water-color competition at the Smithsonian Institute for the Carville (La.) Marine
Hospital, October, 1940; and for the New York State Exhibition at Syracuse in May, 1941.

and buttercups; of bear, deer, and wolves. Art in terms of unheralded, unsung devotion to painting. These were the values to be quietly cherished till the war clouds blew over:

Why does one paint a picture?

Why does one play on a musical instrument?

Is paint strong enough to satisfy the future human eye?

Is the present musical instrument strong enough in sound to satisfy a future demand?

. . . . From the back of my house—up to the woodshed—up to the garage—the turf is wonderfully springy under the feet—it is good to walk on—

The road out from the garage to the end of my place is through a bit of evergreen woodland—and that is mighty good—and—I can imagine—bear—deer—wolves—all sorts of animals a lurking there as they did in the olden time

and that makes it all mighty good and alluring and strange and intimate

The wild roses and the daisies and buttercups which greet us when we come

they are all good—

And———the old men and old women complain—and talk about one who invented automobiles—one who invented the aeroplane—the good old times—

                                        but———

didn't they breed a son who invented Explosives one who invented a something to catch more fish—so that there are now not so many fish to be caught

They complain of a condition they themselves made—didn't they make of it a different world for their sons and daughters to live in and —now they complain of these sons and daughters

Lord—the simple way
if there was ever any such—

they did their best to destroy
Enough of these

            —there be those who have with their doings made for a better world

and I shouldn't wonder but that in many respects—it's a damned sight better world—[12]

---

[12] *Twice A Year* (Fall-Winter 1946–47), letter to Alfred Stieglitz, Addison, Maine, August 10, 1941, pp. 264-5.

The oil seascapes of 1941 quite unexpectedly had a different look, in that the paint was thinned out and areas of unprepared ground were left open—as in his own Castorland paintings of 1913, and in Cézanne's big canvas, the Philadelphia *Bathers,* which he had lately seen and admired. Marin felt that the great work of Cézanne had "lived" long enough to warrant his own further use of unprepared canvas in attempting to see how the white linens could match paper for sparkle. But if it was in his mind to show oils that would gratefully resemble the limpid transparencies, he nevertheless postponed public revelation of that virtuosity: for the droll title of the next exhibition at An American Place was "Pertaining to New York—Circus and Pink Ladies." The pictures that "pertained to New York" were seven paintings of Nassau Street, together with preliminary notes in line and color, while the circus and "pink lady" pictures had been accumulating over the space of three years (Plates 53, 54, 55).[13] Stieglitz was able to list in the March, 1942, catalogue thirteen sets of Marin holdings in important museums.

In 1942, the artist frequently worked in a grove of fir and spruce trees in the Upper Pasture, on the stump-cluttered slope which ascends, through mounds and hollows, from the Cape Split road to his cottage. It was there, for example—sheltered from the winds which blow day and night on the beaches—that he "cooked" (as he says) most of his seascapes in August and September. "The sea on the other side of the trees can't talk back, and if it does, my ears don't hear," he told Stieglitz.[14] One of the seascapes, *Sea and Gulls,* 1942 (Plate 56), received the impasto treatment, but most of the oils of that year were laid down on unprepared canvas with paint almost as thin as light gouache. They were shown in November and the critical public was pleased to allow, here and there, that the oil paintings had begun to equal the water colors in their flowing rhythms.[15]

Marin's son, John Marin IV, was by now in the South Pacific, a noncommissioned officer in the Seventh Aircraft Battalion of the Seventy-seventh Division—the old New York Seventh Regiment. Soldiers encamped on the coast of Washington County tramped over the Cape every day, on guard against landings. The quiet glade in the pasture echoed to the firing of guns over the bay, planes flew low over the beaches near by. Some of the fishermen thought they heard explosions at sea. Marin went quietly on

---

13 Marin commented on the gallery title, *Three Women,* when he first saw it applied to *Three Nudes* at An American Place: "I guess they didn't really look at the picture!"

14 Unpublished letter to Stieglitz, Addison, Maine, September 8, 1942.

15 For example, Henry McBride, New York *Sun* (December 30, 1942), p. 9. Cf. an unsigned review in the New York *Herald-Tribune* (November 7, 1943), section 4, p. 9.

I. Boats, Sea and Rocks, 1943 (oil)

with his work, suppressing anxiety for the sake of his wife, who was already failing in health. He was painting more and more now out of his memory. He was seventy-two; feeling kind of seedy. . . .

Perhaps in an attempt to live up to his title, "Leprechaun on the Palisades," [16] he spent a good part of the following winter making imaginative drawings of nudes—reluctant, like Cézanne, to use the live model (Plate 57). There is a sheaf of thirty pencil studies on cellophane: variations—one might have called them musical variations—on the theme of two female nude figures. The fundamental design remains constant throughout, the treatment varies from the round likeness to geometric abstraction. Marin was "fooling around" irresistibly, but with what masterful fooling!

Returning to Cape Split to spend the summer of 1943—and occupying, "in spite of the wars," the "Ancient Mariner's lookout"—he took comfort from nature as he thought of his son, now in dangerous territory. "The little purple and gold asters in clumps . . . beautiful (the earth is beautiful). If only those who live on it would behave." As for health, he was once more "feeling his Oats." As for painting, he wrote that he had given it up: "I just tie a brush to my finger and let that silly old brush do the painting," [17] he said (Plate I). That autumn in the Franconia Range in New Hampshire, the silly old brush produced some water colors that were remarkable for containing the purest essence of Marin.

In 1944, the Marins—neither one in good health that year—stayed on at Cape Split until the end of October, burning wood in the kitchen stove to save rationed fuel oil at home. "A few pictures painted—that is if you can call them pictures," Marin reported.[18] As a matter of fact, you could quite easily call them pictures; good pictures, although somewhat tricky. The seascapes are preoccupied with the middle horizon, which begins at the base of an inverted pyramidal structure—a not infrequent element in the Marin design. But there were not many of these, nor of the romantic swamp landscapes; [19] the number of pictures required for a new exhibition

---

[16] Matthew Josephson, *New Yorker* (March 14, 1942), pp. 26-32. The term was first Rosenfeld's.

[17] Letter to Stieglitz, Cape Split, Maine, September 29, 1943, printed in the exhibition catalogue of November 5, 1943-January 9, 1944, and reprinted in *Twice A Year* (Fall-Winter 1946–47), p. 265.

[18] Unpublished letter to Stieglitz, Cape Split, October 19, 1944.

[19] One of the water colors in a set of seven representative Marins assembled by Mr. and Mrs. Clifford Odets is *Swamp Maple* of 1944. This was not the first Marin, however, to join the Paul Klee collection in the Odets' California villa. Their first purchase, in 1945, was a New Mexican landscape of 1930, later paired with another of 1929. Their earliest Marin, *Tidal Falls*, is a Deer Isle picture of 1923; their favorite Marin, *Green Head*, was made on Deer Isle in the following summer. The remaining three aquarelles "pertain" to Cape Split.

was made up at home, with a series of late-season studies of autumn woods in New Jersey and some "drawings" on canvas (Plate 58).

The catalogue for the winter showing called "Painting—1944" announced an oil portrait of Mrs. Marin; but since it was made while the painter's wife, then mortally ill, was barely clinging to life, the artist withheld it. She died on her birthday, March 1, 1945, at the house in Cliffside. Her husband was with her, her son half a world distant. She was buried in a new plot of ground in the Fairview Cemetery, in Fairview, New Jersey, a town adjacent to Cliffside. Marin was past seventy-four when he lost her. For thirty years she had shared his life, kept his house, cut his hair, gone everywhere with him. There are no letters which have passed between them; they were rarely apart.

One of Mrs. Marin's Cape Split friends speaks of her "sweet timidity." A small, birdlike person, she dressed often in gray. She had hazel eyes, dark brown hair which was only slightly grayed when she died, and sensitive, life-worn hands. Her face, quiet, almost severe, in repose, would light up at the sight of her family and friends. Content with the out-of-door life in which she followed her husband, she had decided likes and dislikes in respect to society. Fond as she was of her few hearthside friends, she hated snobbishness and hypocrisy. She was not always sure that she knew what her husband had to say in his pictures, but she had a good eye for balance. "That picture don't seem to me to weigh right, John," she would say, once or twice in a season, and Marin would sometimes have to admit that she was correct in her judgment.

Except at the Cape, Marin now had little society. "I never went out much with people," he says. Since John Marin, Jr., who formerly took his father to plays and the circus and the boxing arena, was then on the Island of Leyte, in training for the invasion of the Ryukyu Islands, Marin felt sadly alone. He turned to his well-thumbed Nelson Shakespeare and wrote letters to his friends at the Cape. He told Mrs. Thompson that he longed to return to Cape Split. "Enjoy the beautiful earth while it is there to enjoy," he said to the Thompsons. "It's our resting place."

It was with many misgivings that he drove Down East in August, with a friend and legal adviser who spent a month with him. Paul Strand joined him at the Cape for a part of September and encouraged him to go on with his work. The oil paintings were austere, problematical (Plate 59). The water colors, however, show Marin thinking less of pictorial problems than of the beautiful earth. He showed how it looked. And when the weather grew cold and he returned to Cliffside alone, there reposed in the back of his car one of the most romantic landscapes of his entire career—a canvas,

Machias, Maine, in which the Longfellow town of Machias seemed to nestle, as a Cape neighbor put it, in the right hand of God (Plate 60).

The end of the ravage of time, as another year proved, was not yet. Alfred Stieglitz, Marin's patron and confidant for more than thirty-five years, died on July 13, 1946, age eighty-two—a gallant old man full of years and of personal triumphs.

Many voices, some of them sounding shrill and loud to dispassionate ears, had long piped to his tune. A bible had been compiled in his honor from the works of twenty-five writers from Saint John the Evangelist to Miss Gertrude Stein. Furthermore, he was always well able to speak for himself, and according to legend talked copiously to the end of his life. Yet it appears that his genius was not always persuasive; for while his coterie confessed him a saint, the world sometimes expressed wonder.

What was Stieglitz after? That is what skeptics wondered. It seemed he was not after money. His artists believed him when he said that he never augmented his private resources from gallery profits. He was after power, some thought, and power he had in abundance in the world that he lived in. He had to be all in all to his worshipers; any lapse from strict monotheism was punishable, as Edmund Wilson has noted, by instant excommunication. Sometimes his painters lived and died in the faith; others remained in the darkness, abandoned by friends and scorned by the critics who clung to the creed of the master.[20]

In one episode in the Stieglitz annals, young Alfred is disclosed in the midst of his elders.[21] But unlike the young hero of an older gospel, preoccupied, it is said, with his father's business, the boy from the dark-room is distinctly bent upon affairs of his own: such as raising money for mythical monkeys. Continuing all his life in the character of the youth at Lake George, Stieglitz collected coins for the monkeys he sheltered; yet he confessed to his mother, reminiscing one day in his fifties, that he never really gave anything to anyone but himself.

I was reminded, on my first visit to Stieglitz, around 1935, of Irvin Cobb's story of a baseball game to which a governor of the state of New Jersey was escorted by a fluttering aide. The aide in Cobb's story hovers over His Excellency all afternoon, bobbing and bowing and superintending. "It was," Cobb reported, "as though the governor had been an egg and the gentleman had laid him." So one got the impression that the pictures one saw at An American Place were Stieglitz's eggs, not O'Keeffe's,

---

[20] Edmund Wilson, "Paul Rosenfeld: Three Phases," in *Paul Rosenfeld, Voyager in the Arts,* edited by Jerome Mellquist and Lucie Wiese (New York, 1948), p. 7.
[21] Paul Rosenfeld, "The Boy in the Dark-Room," *America and Alfred Stieglitz,* Chapter III.

91

Dove's, or Marin's. Some of the eggs were put on the market and dozens of others were put down in water-glass in Stieglitz's private collection: above two hundred first-rate water colors by Marin alone, together with scores of Demuths, Doves, and Hartleys.

Since the known facts of Marin's once restricted economy raise the question of the circumstances under which Stieglitz came into possession of so many pictures, I asked Mr. Marin to explain what had happened. I pass on what he told me. When the painter and Stieglitz went over the paintings which were hung year by year on the walls of whatever gallery, Stieglitz would ask Marin to name the lowest price he would take for each picture. These prices were set down in writing. Then—quite rightly, thought Marin—Stieglitz would make his own choice at the minimum prices, which were small in the days when the collection was forming, and advance, when he could, the price asked from the public. Sometimes Stieglitz sold from his private collection, sending the proceeds to Marin and then making replacements with newer pictures on the basis of Marin's own prices—perhaps getting three new paintings in return for the one he had sold. Marin took what came in all gratitude, feeling that his patron's intention was generous: for Stieglitz was, after all, saving fine pictures to go into museum collections.

One of Stieglitz's friends describes the process of buying and selling when spirit (as buyer and seller are called) met shining spirit at An American Place: "It is more a passionate exchange rather than the age-old idea of trading. The difference lies in the approach. If . . . the buyer seeks earnestly a means to meet the demand made for the artist, then, with the welfare of the artist always in mind, Stieglitz advances to meet the buyer; acknowledging the spirit of the buyer and his or her fitness to possess the painting. Thus the passionate exchange is made, and Stieglitz's lifelong endeavor to procure a decent livelihood for the artist momentarily accomplished." [22]

In a letter of February 15, 1944, in the author's possession, Stieglitz speaks of a "rent fund," a "contribution" which was deducted from the purchase price of a picture. In the early years of the Marin and Stieglitz relationship, as the letters however show, there seems to have been a franker conception between them of financial matters. The earliest recorded letter

---

[22] Dorothy Brett, "The Room," *America and Alfred Stieglitz* (Copyright 1934 by Doubleday & Company, Inc.), p. 261. For further commentary on Stieglitz's fiscal arrangements, see the correspondence between Mrs. Dorothy Norman and MacKinley Helm in *The Atlantic Monthly* (May, 1947), and the article, "Alfred Stieglitz," by James Thrall Soby, *Saturday Review of Literature* (September 28, 1946), pp. 22 f.

from painter to patron, written aboard the SS. *Nieuw Amsterdam* on May 18, 1910, when Marin was on his way home from Europe, brings up the matter of the payment of $100 by a Dutch buyer for two water colors bespoken at the 1909 show in New York. "You spoke about a few dollars coming to me," wrote Marin. "Will you kindly deduct *that which goes to the Photo-Secession* on these 2 sales from [that] amount."

"Stieglitz was a strange man, but he fought for Marin to his dying day," writes a Marin collector. For instance, as noted in a personal letter, he protected his artists by selling their pictures into what the trade calls "strong hands." And it is true that relatively few of Marin's paintings have found their way to the auctions, where established price structures can collapse in a single untoward evening. But the chief testimonial to the value of Stieglitz's guardianship comes from Marin himself, who, when I have seemed to be critical of one of the most perplexing arrangements in art's curious history, has always concluded, "You can say what you will, Stieglitz has always left me alone when it came to my work."

The Ancient Mariner

Fall, 1946—1948

WHEN I PAID MY FIRST CALL ON THE PAINTER, IN THE year of Stieglitz's death, I walked with some friends down a lane of blue spruce connecting Cape Split with "Windslip," [1] the house where I stayed. We passed the burial ground of Jason Look's family, old settlers who had once lived at "Windslip"; crossed the bar which narrowly connects the Cape with the mainland; and walked up a road bordered by lilac-pink butterfly bush and red bunch berries. Then we turned up a rough track through an ascending wood lot to a clearing, crossed the Upper Pasture, and approached the glassed-in verandah of a white bayside cottage. Marin, convalescent from a severe heart attack, was playing the first of Bach's *Two-Part Inventions* on the old-fashioned Chickering. His lively hands chased each other over the keyboard and his thin shoulders moved with the quick play of phrase against phrase.

"That is the kind of music my piano likes to have played on it," he said, when he discovered us there. "That music is full of movement and life. Did you hear how the little tunes struck at each other? That is an example of balance and force."

As he warmly invited us in to stay for the sunset, his smiling eyes and small, wrinkled mouth, beneath the gray curls and bangs, reminded me of what Marsden Hartley once said about him: "There is always a play of earthly humor about to fall like an autumn leaf from his face."

"Can you promise us a real Marin sunset?" I asked.

"I think it will be a mighty fine sunset," he replied, looking out upon Pleasant Bay from the multiwindowed verandah. And as a matter of fact, it turned out to be the most glittering sunset of the early fall season.

As the sun began to go down behind the Tunk Mountains and the headlands beyond Dyer's Island, west of Cadillac Mountain—all disposed as in Marin's paintings—the painter excused himself from the talk.

"I want to make notes of this sunset," he said. "It is really something quite out of the ordinary."

Since he was sketching, and not painting a picture, he allowed me to

---

[1] To "slip your wind," in the Maine idiom, means "to die."

94

watch. He worked on an 8″ x 10″ pad in his lap, a paint box on a wooden chair seat before him, a porcelain bowl filled with water on a table near by. With his right hand he roughed in, with black crayon, the three elements of the picture—sky, headland, and bay; and laid on the color with furious strokes of a half-inch brush in his left hand. His hands fought each other over the paper as they had done while he played the *Two-Part Invention.*

The sunset colors changed rapidly. A feathery patch of red cloud became purple, the purple thinned out to show a red lining. A sky passage turned acid yellow even while Marin laid a mixture of yellow ocher and cadmium on the dry painting surface. A dull robin's-egg blue became brilliant turquoise.

"See that blue spot out there?" Marin said, dabbing impatiently. "That's a 'light' color. You can't put it on paper. You can't even get it with mixtures of color—viridian, cerulean, French blue, chromium oxide green, or what have you. So you just put down a color that the paper will like, a color that looks all right in itself. If the paper likes it, it doesn't matter if it's not a transcript from nature.

"Sometimes," he went on, "I like to paint a red ocean, with light red, maybe, between Venetian and Indian red, or maybe spectrum red. . . . Red is more exciting than gray. . . . It is not the color that makes a painted ocean look like a real ocean. . . . What makes the painted ocean look real is a suggestion of the motion of water. . . . A red ocean with motion will look more like the sea than a patch of gray paint without movement."

He told me that one of his most persistent collectors is a color-blind personage who visits the Cliffside studio and has bought dozens of small water colors. This curious circumstance seemed to the painter to prove that the transcription of motion from nature is more important to the truthfulness of a painting than the literal transference of color.

His "notes" well laid down by the time darkness drew in, Marin spoke of the connection between his painting and music. "I don't know any big musical words," he explained. "All I know about music I have learned by myself. But I think that Haydn and Bach and those fellows before Haydn's time—those English fellows like Purcell and Orlando Gibbons—gave their music real action. I try to make the parts of my pictures move the same way, only I always try to make them move back and forth from the center of the paper or canvas—like notes leaving and going back to middle C on the keyboard.

"I take my skiff and row out to one of the islands, Sheep Island, Eagle Island, Norton Island, out there in the bay in front of my house," he went on. "I see rocks upriver and the water flowing. All right, I put down the

95

rocks on my paper. Then I show how the water runs past the rocks. The water is more white than colored, you notice, but you have to use color—never mind what color—or you couldn't show how the water runs along on white paper. Now, I say to myself, the most important thing about a river is that it runs downhill past the rocks. Simple, isn't it?"

And it is true that Marin's pictures seemed simpler to look at when one saw, at first hand, how truly the painter is nature's own child; how tinctured his speech with the poetic details of nature's appearance. Whether at home on the Cape, or on the offshore islands (Outer Sand, Crumple, Jordan's Delight), or in the interior, towards Tunk Half Way and the village of Centerville, Marin lives from sunrise to dark in communion with nature. He knows the movement of clouds, the direction of wind, the ebb and flow of the tides. He makes friends with swamps and beaches, trees and flowers, birds and beasts—everything that has life and structure. As in the middle of the nineteenth century, another great American artist, Henry David Thoreau, traveling with his traps in a paper parcel, examined the beaches along another cape and wrote a pair of colored chapters in *Cape Cod,* the lovely, slighted sister of his *Walden,* so Marin, conversely using color, produces by indirect intention a nearly verbal thesaurus of the natural events of his own Downeastern cape.

"Art is produced by the wedding of man and nature," he had said in one of his letters. "When man loves material and will not under any circumstances destroy its own inherent beauty, then and then only can that wonderful thing we call art be created." [2] So it is that for every rule in his painting, he can produce a likeness from nature.

"Take the idea of balance," he says. "Think of the wonderful balance of squirrels. They scratch themselves equally well with hind paws or fore paws without losing their balance. When I have put down enough things to cover the surface, I like my pictures to have that kind of balance. I stand them up on their end, turn them upside down, until I see that, like the squirrels, they have got balance in every direction." [3]

In a note composed as a preface to the publication of some of his later letters, Marin bade painters to "go look at the bird's flight, the man's walk, the sea's movement. They have a way to keep their motion. Nature's laws of motion have to be obeyed and you have to follow along— The good picture embraces these laws—the best of the old did—that's what gives them life." [4]

---

[2] Unpublished letter to Stieglitz, Addison, Maine, August 31, 1940.

[3] *See* Paul Rosenfeld, "An Essay on Marin," *The Nation* (January 27, 1932), p. 122, for further study of equilibrium in Marin's paintings.

[4] *Twice A Year* (Spring-Summer 1939), p. 176.

Marin was preoccupied then, as throughout his career, with the balance of color as well as the balance of forms. Except when he "plays around," as he says, with two colors, trying to see how nearly he can get the effect of a third hue without overtly using it, he expresses nature's balance of color in the three primary hues, red, blue, and yellow.

"Nature reveals herself in sets of three things," he says. "There is land between sky and water, gray between black and white, lukewarm between hot and cold, the diagonal between the upright and prone."

Sometimes he lets black stand for red,[5] sometimes leaves it up to the spectator to see the red casts in ocher or the hints of yellow contained in light red and cerulean blue. But the three primary hues must be present, he thinks, in one way or another, to make the balance of color complete. "Nature has given them to us," he said. "How can we get rid of them? None of them is absent from nature except when nature is sick." Consistently, he likes old American flags better than new ones because in the old ones the white has turned yellow.

Even for the most difficult phase of his art, the creation of planes of color and atmosphere on the flat surface of paper or canvas, Marin has found a happy likeness in nature. Earth and sea are ideally (and pictorially) flat, he observes. When the surface of ocean is disturbed by a storm, the waves rising high, troughs scooped out of the depths, the artist remembers the flatness to which the sea must return. And while he paints the storm, he puts in a reference to the calm into which the storm must resolve. Similarly, he sees how, with the passing of geological time, hills are raised up and leveled, valleys dug out and filled, as though nature were trying to preserve her equilibrium on a flat plane. So in the landscapes, the flatness of earth is portrayed, whatever else happens. The subject matter itself is either flatly handled or subjoined to flat, rectangular areas; and usually the paper is left exposed at the edges, as a frame of reference—flat in itself and representative of the flatness of earth.

As a painter strongly addicted to painting, and never surprised, like Cézanne, to learn, late in life, the difference between painting and sculpture, Marin says that his most serious professional problem is to "get a picture to travel on its planes." What he means, really, is that when a painter puts several "views" into one picture, it is difficult to keep them detached from the great fixed, flat plane of the surface, so that they can live, breathe, and move and yet not interfere with each other. Suppose, for example, that he paints a house in front of a valley in front of a mountain—and leaves holes,

---

[5] An "impressionistic" effect usually revealed only to the trained sensibility which can see inferred tones of color in shadows.

so to speak, in the forward view of the house and in that of the valley so that the mountain shows through and so that each of the views may receive its own air to breathe in. The artist who thinks in these terms is not satisfied with a picture until each view is complete in itself; so that if he chose to "lift off" any one of them, what remained would be whole and complete; or if he lifted the whole, the surface would still be intact.

This highly theoretical and metaphorical conception is likewise the spectator's most serious problem; but when it is mastered, it explains much fine painting since Tintoretto. The spectator may find it helpful, in thinking of much "modern" painting, to remember that the flat surface of earth is turned, in a painting, into a vertical—up-and-down—plane. Against that vertical plane of the earth, the figures which exist on any one plane of the picture, whether they are abstract or real, whether triangles or mountains or people, whether single objects or groups of objects, will seem to recede or come forward, to move in and out, if—like Tintoretto, Cézanne, and Marin—the painter has been thinking in terms of the flat surface of earth and canvas and paper. It is this kind of motion which keeps a painting alive.

The relation between art and nature was the theme of a Note composed for the catalogue of a Marin exhibition which was opened at the Institute of Contemporary Art, Boston, on January 7, 1947, with a retrospective showing of nineteen oils, forty-five water colors, twenty-odd drawings, and twelve etchings, and was thereafter hung at the Phillips Memorial Gallery in Washington, D. C., and the Walker Art Center in Minneapolis. Clothing his thought in rent and spangled raiment, Marin reaffirmed his faith in those familiar antonyms, art's dependence on nature and independence of fact:

> *Is not a work of art [he wrote from Cliffside], the most tantalizing—here—there—where—yes and no—sort of thing on Earth—the most vital, yet to all a mystery—to not too many a mysterious reality—it cannot be understood, it can be felt.*
>
> *. . . . to be looked at with a looking eye—with a looking eye of many lookings—to see as it slowly reveals itself the process of the revealing—to such giving infinite pleasure, this individual—the artist—releasing the different folds of his seeings at periods of his many livings.*
>
> *He—be he working on a flat surface reforms his seeings on this surface to a seeing of his own choosing so that which he chooses shall live of its own right on this flat—*
>
> *The flat—the symbol of the soil and upon this soil—upright—the plant agrowing and living.*
>
> *. . . . so as in great nature—the soil not to lose its identity, the plant*

not to have its nature killed—and on the soil and amongst the plants—there'll be stones—there'll be weeds—that's life— Leave it to the true creative artist—he'll find a place for the stones and weeds of life in his picture and all so arranged that each takes its place and part in that rhythmic whole—that balanced whole—to sing its music with color, line and spacing upon its keyboard.

. . . . the picture appears—a work of art tells the story the best, it transcends the factual.

Shakespeare's lines 'Full fathom five thy father lies, of his bones are coral made' can be factually told by anybody but who can tell it the way Shakespeare tells it—it's the artist speaking—so that to the artist it's the way of the telling always that concerns him: the painter his way, the sculptor his. The material used—the way used—of a verity—that's the story.

Meeting new people in Boston, and old friends in Washington, Marin was happy to learn of the pleasure which his pictures so clearly gave to so many (though not all!) of the thousands of people who saw them. He spoke, on his visit to Boston, of providing, as so many modern painters have failed to, for a bridge between painter and public. This was a problem which had occupied his mind for many years; for as long ago as 1928 he had said to the late Edward Alden Jewell, "I am forced to pit my horse sense against yours. Otherwise there would be no race, no fun." In the "race" between artist and spectator, the more equal the entries, the more exciting the aesthetic experience. When the horses gallop together, he seemed to imply, the excitement is nearly complete.

The painter, to be sure, must be allowed his fair place in the handicap. He must be permitted to *be* a painter, not a story-teller: to "show paint as paint" on the flat paper or canvas with which he begins. But he ought to give pleasure if he proposes to show his work to the public, just as the musician, playwright, or novelist intends to give pleasure. Marin supposes that the painter who gives the most pleasure, by whatever system of measurement, is the one who loves paint and does not hate subject matter. Let an artist observe those conditions and then let him find his own style. Any one of a million styles—if there were a million painters enamored with subject and paint—could give pleasure. This is both Marin's warning to painters and counsel to patrons.

Judging other painters on their adherence to their objective visions of nature and their affection for paint, Marin prefers Van Gogh to Gauguin because Van Gogh had a more passionate feeling for the material world. He commends Mondrian for his rediscovery of "two facts of life," namely horizontal and vertical motion; but he thinks Mondrian left out the life which goes on in nature around the lines which go up and down and across. He likes the pictures of Maurice Prendergast and Marsden Hartley, both of whom had sincere visions of nature's vitality which they rendered with love. Of the old masters, he prefers Tintoretto to Titian. "You can copy a Titian," he says, "but how could you copy a Tintoretto? Tintoretto's nervous tensions cannot be imitated. Tintoretto just about fills the bill."

He admires Goya, who seems to him not so much to have copied nature's creations as to have created freshly in paint after nature's example. And he likes old Dutch paintings of flowers because of the tenderness with which precious objects were handled. Among his own paintings, the 1946 series of six water colors descriptive of a Saddle River (New Jersey) peach orchard in bloom illustrated this doctrine about as closely as anything could. The peach trees, looking like ballet dancers swaying to music, give out to the spectator the greatest amount of communicable pleasure and joy, and at the same time were admittedly delightful to paint.

There were twenty-nine new paintings to show at An American Place in April, 1947, as the result of Marin's work during his seventy-sixth year: eight water-color landscapes including the Saddle River peach-orchard series; seven water-color seascapes; five landscapes in oil including two views of the Tunk Mountains; and nine sea "movements," also in oil. The year's portfolio was a recapitulation in miniature of Marin's lifetime habit of work: the yielding, in moments of transport, to the direct impulse, the capturing of a look and an atmosphere; and the long, lonely ascent to the rarefied, intellectual level with its preoccupation with the accents of paint. The two versions of *On the Road to Addison, Maine,* painted towards the end of the summer, showed him engaged with the problems of "making a painting to travel on its own planes. . . ."

The following summer began with a honeymoon. John Marin, Jr. married Grace Clark Morley, a Vassar girl from Weehawken, on July 12, at Grove Church, New Durham, the Dutch Reformed parish of which Marin's great-grandfather, James Gardner, had been one of the founders. The young couple, remembering that the painter had suffered a severe heart attack in Cliffside following Stieglitz's death, invited him to go along on the wedding trip. They went *à trois* to St. Hubert's, on the East Branch of the Ausable River in the high Adirondacks, so that Marin could show his daughter-in-law the mountain country he painted the summer before his own marriage.

Using a palette composed principally of greens and blues for the midsummer foliage, Marin painted the mountains in the Keene Valley region, which runs north of St. Hubert's toward Au Sable Forks. Most of the paintings were typical early-season impromptus and *études*, although in the last one, *Whiteface Mountain*, made just east of Lake Placid, the subject matter was broken up into a series of planes related to the flat plane of the surface. When I spoke of the moist look of the nine Ausable washes, seeing them at Cape Split one day in August, Marin explained that it had rained nearly the whole time he had spent in the mountains. One of the water colors, *Looking West on Ausable River*, had been painted, indeed, just at the outbreak of a heavy downpour.

The Marins then drove on to Cape Split, where, the young people thought, Marin was sure to be happier and more at home. During the fall at the Cape, he produced five water colors and ten oil paintings, fulfilling a promise he had made to himself, now that he was getting on to seventy-seven, to paint as he chose; for himself, if need be. He had one thing in mind, he explained—"to give paint a chance to show itself entirely as paint."

"Using paint *as* paint," he said, "is different from using paint to paint a picture. I'm calling my pictures this year 'Movements in Paint' and not movements of boat, sea, or sky, because in these new paintings, although I use objects, I am representing paint first of all, and not the motif primarily."

A day on the bay provided a perfect occasion for one of the "Movements in Paint." The Marin family and the "Windslip" household had gone fishing one morning in Marin's old lobster boat, out across Pleasant Bay and past rocky Flint Island; and on the way back in the late afternoon, Marin pointed out an unusual color effect on the water. To starboard, the water was of a ruddy blue cast, while the sky over it was a bright, clear blue. To larboard, the sea was green under a cold gray sky. "This is something no painter could paint," I remarked, "no one would believe him." Marin used the motif in the oil painting, *Movement in Paint* (Plate 61). There are the two seas on the canvas, side by side; green on the left, blue flecked with red on the right, the gray sky above the green sea, a blue sky above the blue sea, and a red disk in between. It is an entirely successful theoretical painting, for it is exciting in its very exposition of paint.

Three of the new seascapes were made with a palette of light red and cobalt green, strengthened with white, green *composé*, and stitches of black. They were intended to show how paint can rise up and come at you or recede into the distance. Among the more memorable and beguiling 1947 paintings are two seascapes, one with pink (light red) sky, pink ship, and two pink figures, a female nude and a fish, set in rectangles in a blue sea (Plate 62); and the other with a turbulent sea, white waves, and Mrs.

101

Thompson in blue on the rocks at the right. The latter *Movement in Paint* (Plate 63), which might have been called *The White Wave,* clearly ranks with the masterpieces, the "homers" which Marin has knocked out not infrequently. The series concluded with a large abstract landscape executed in a complicated pattern of planes. "I am going to call it *Sea or Mountain As You Will,*" Marin said. "The paint is the thing."

Two of the five 1947 aquarelles, *Flint Island No. 1* and *Flint Island No. 2,* attacked the problem of movement in paint with the transparent colors. In the first, the paint seems to rise up and the spectator looks *down* into the seascape. In the second, the paint recedes into the vertical plane of the paper and one looks *over* the sea. Then, since the season would have seemed incomplete without at least one nontheoretical poem, Marin made a farewell view from Outer Sand Island, a sheerly poetical monochromatic *étude* in blue, with touches of light red and ocher on a cliffside in the background and blacks in the foreground.

On the road into Boston in October, to pay a brief visit on his way back to Cliffside, Marin caught sight of the Longfellow Bridge, locally known, for the turrets, as the Pepperpot Bridge. He liked the way the long span of arches came to an end—so it seemed—at Beacon Hill on the Boston side of Charles River. We went back to the Cambridge end of the bridge for some sketching next morning and Marin once more obliged me by letting me watch the process by which he arrives at his more abstract conclusions: the process which Cézanne is supposed to have gone through in his head and so denied to his followers the pleasure of seeing the intermediate stages. Three sketches of the arched and turreted masonry bridge spanned the process of recording and "playing around." In the last theoretical drawing, the city of Boston lay flattened out in irregular polygons radiating over the paper from a base at the end of the bridge. One felt that one saw, for the first time in one's life, how a familiar landscape was really composed beneath the raw surface view and how that deep look was the true subject for art.

I was reminded of a conversation I had had with Mrs. Charles Bittinger, when she told me how Marin, thirty-five years ago, used to sketch a motif over and over again to try to capture its movement and feeling. One day, when they were walking together along the North River, Marin climbed to a perilous perch on a parapet and made ten or twelve rapid sketches of railway tracks paralleling the river. "Don't you see," he had cried, as he tore up the drawings, "how those black tracks race to keep up with the current?"

". . . . Do you see what I'm doing?" Marin now asked, gazing across the Charles River to Boston. "I am relating the view to my paper. When the view on top of the paper begins to recede, it returns to the paper I am putting it down on." What it seemed to come down to was that the artist had ruled out illusion as a means to aesthetic ends. Here was art in its purity. One thought of the Gospel Beatitudes; one thought, "This man will see God. . . ."

And so we take leave of the artist—the poet and theorist—in the seventy-eighth year of his life, his earthly, autumn-leaf humor intact, his art ripe but firm, his family life once more secure, his thoughts harking back to Cape Split: not in time but in space; for in time lies a precious future of painting.

Faithful neighbors there have been contented for years to take him to be what he is, a plain, boylike man who carries a polished stone in his pocket, worries about the animals when he sees smoke in the forests, and unaccountably makes his living by painting instead of by fishing. The Thompsons have always cherished the letters from Cliffside signed "The Ancient Mariner," but until lately they never knew much about his life off the Cape. They never knew he was famous and "comfortably off" until one of the neighbors saw a magazine piece about An American Place and showed it around. And it was startling to hear, some months later, that critics referred to him as "America's No. 1 Master," while a national magazine poll placed him at the top of the list of great living American painters.[6] They learned with surprise—he would not have told them—that a single picture sometimes fetched the price of a new lobster boat.

When it came, however, the revelation made no great difference in Cape Split's friendly feelings. His friends still like the painter best as plain Mr. Marin when they welcome him to their kitchens to sit for an evening. Sometimes there are concerts, when Mr. Wass plays the fiddle down at his daughter's. Most of the time, one sits in the cookroom—Marin, comfortable in a gray cardigan jacket and tan cotton trousers, sitting at ease in a red rocking chair; Bill Thompson, beside the lamp at the end of the table, knitting balls of green twine into heads and bait pockets for the lobster pots. A little talk, a short nap, a hot cup of tea . . . all relaxed and affectionate.

One makes out that the Thompsons never pester the painter with the talk that he hears in New York about whether he is an impressionist, abstractionist, realist. In his own mind, he remains realist, consistently creating his paintings from the natural forms. "The sea that I paint may not be *the* sea, but it is *a* sea, not an abstraction," he says. Mrs. Thompson caught a glimpse of his meaning while he was painting her portrait. "His hands," she declared, "looked as though they were trying to force some new creation up from the canvas, as nature pushes a sprout through the earth and creates a new tree."

---

[6] *LOOK* (February 3, 1948), p. 44.

John Marin

"His pictures do grow on you," said Bill Thompson one evening, reaffirming the outside world's opinion as he cut a whore's-egg thorn from his finger. "But sometimes I have to tell John that a boat must *look* like a boat—not, you know, just *go* like a boat as some say. I say, 'John, a man has to haul fish from those boats.' " And Marin agrees that art ought to show where it takes off from the earth.

Plates

1. *Miss Lelia Currey at the Piano (drawing)*   *page* 107

2. *Cour Dragon, Paris, 1906 (etching)*   *page* 109

3. *Street Scene, Paris, 1907 (etching)*   *page* 111

4. *London Omnibus, 1908 (water color)*   *page* 113

5. *Pont Alexandre, 1909 (water color)* page 115

6. *Four O'Clock on the Seine, 1909 (water color)*   *page* 117

7. *Chartres Cathedral, 1910 (etching)*   *page* 119

8. *Tyrol at Kufstein, Tyrol Series, No. 3, 1910 (water color)*   *page* 121

9. *The Mountain, Tyrol, 1910 (water color)*   *page* 123

10.   *Woolworth Building, No. 31, 1912 (water color)*   *page* 125

11. *Woolworth Building, No. 3, 1913 (etching)*   *page* 127

12. *Marin Island, Maine, 1915 (water color)*   *page* 129

13.　*Delaware (River) Country, Pennsylvania, 1916 (water color)*　　*page* 131

14. *Sunset, Casco Bay, 1919 (water color)*   *page* 133

15. *Lower Manhattan from the River, No. 2, 1921 (water color)*   *page* 135

16. *Village, Maine, 1923 (water color)*   *page* 137

17. *Two-master Becalmed, Maine, 1923 (water color)*   *page* 139

18. *Deer Isle, Stonington, Maine, 1924 (water color)*   *page* 141

19. *Downtown New York, 1925 (etching)*   *page* 143

20.   *Movement, Boat and Sea, Deer Isle, Maine, 1927 (water color)*   *page* 145

21. *Pertaining to Deer Isle—the Harbor, 1927 (water color)*   *page* 147

22. *White Mountains, Autumn, 1927 (water color)*   *page* 149

23. *A Southwester, 1928 (water color)*   *page* 151

24. *Boat Fantasy, Deer Isle, 1928 (water color)* *page* 153

25. *Midtown, New York, 1928 (water color)*   *page* 155

26.   *Street Crossing, New York, 1928 (water color)*   *page* 157

27. *Broadway, Night, 1929 (water color)*   *page* 159

28. *Taos Landscape, New Mexico, 1929 (water color)*   *page* 161

29. *Pueblo and Mesa, Taos Mountains, 1929 (water color)*   *page* 163

30. *Blue Mountain Near Taos, 1929 (water color)*   *page* 165

31. *Dance of the San Domingo Indians, 1929*   *page 167*

32. *Stonington Harbor, 1931 (water color)* page 169

33. *Rocks and Sea, Small Point, Maine, 1931 (oil)*   *page* 171

34.   *Looking up Fifth Avenue from 30th Street, 1932 (oil)*   *page* 173

35. *Deep-Sea Trawlers, Maine, 1932 (oil)*   *page* 175

36. *Composition, Cape Split, 1933 (oil)*   *page* 177

37.   *Tree, No. 1, Cape Split, Maine Coast, 1933 (water color)*   *page* 179

38.   *Fishing Boat, No. 2, 1933 (water color)*   *page* 181

39.   *Women Forms and Sea, 1934 (oil)*   *page* 183

40.   *Lake, Tunk Mountain, Maine Series, No. 12, 1934 (water color)*   *page* 185

41. *Young Man of the Sea, Maine Series, No. 10, 1934 (water color)*   *page* 187

42. *East River, No. 3, 1934 (water color)*   *page* 189

43. *From Seeing Cape Split, 1935 (oil)*   *page* 191

44. *Circus Horses, 1936 (oil)*   *page* 193

45. *Sea Gulls, No. 2, 1936 (water color)*   *page* 195

46. *New York, East River, 1936 (water color)*   *page* 197

47. *New York, Downtown, 1936 (water color)* page 199

48.   *Off Cape Split, 1937 (water color)*   *page* 201

49. *Sea with Red Sky, 1937 (oil)*   *page* 203

50. *Four Bathers, 1937 (drawing)*   *page* 205

51. *Laurel Blossoms in Vase, 1938 (oil)*   *page 207*

52.   *Lobster Boat, 1940 (oil)*   *page* 209

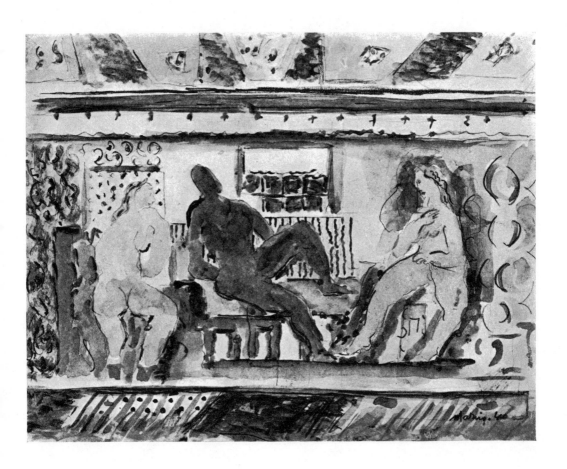

53. *Three Nudes, 1940 (water color)*   *page* 211

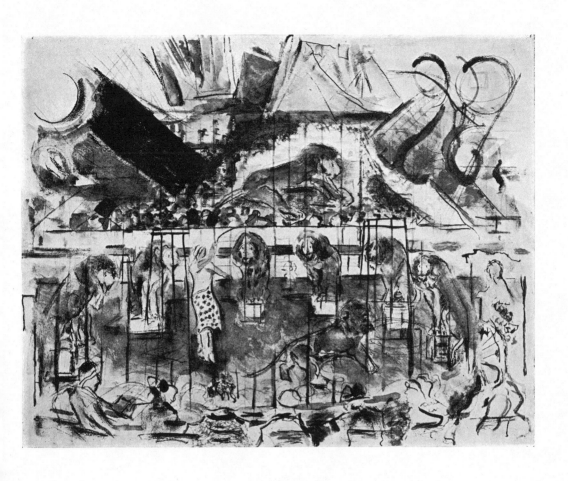

54. *In the Ring, 1941 (water color)* *page* 213

55.   *Circus Ring, Horses, 1941 (drawing)*   *page* 215

56.   *Sea and Gulls, 1942 (oil)*   *page 217*

7. *Bathers on Rocks, 1943 (water color)* page 219

58. *Equestrienne, 1944 (oil)* *page* 221

Boat with Blue, 1945 (oil)   *page* 223

60. *Machias, Maine, 1945 (oil)*   *page* 225

61. *Movement in Paint, 1947 (oil)*   *page 227*

62.   *Movement in Paint, 1947 (oil)*   *page* 229

63. *Movement in Paint, 1947 (oil)*<space count="36" />*page* 231

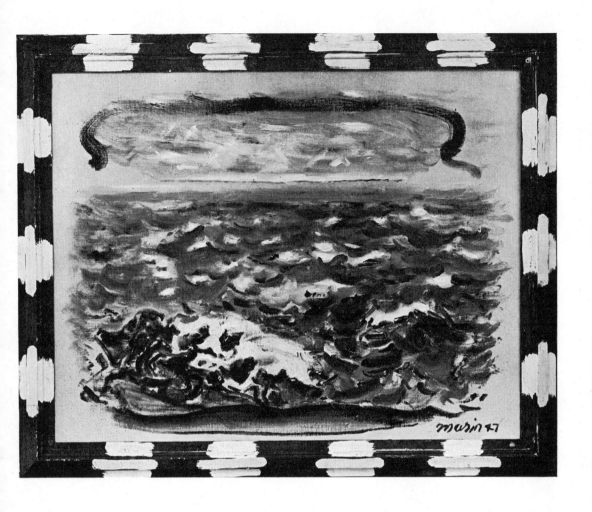

64. *Movement in Paint, 1947 (oil)* *page* 233

Index

Thoreau, Henry David, 75, 96
Tintoretto, Jacopo Robusti, 16, 98, 100
Titian (Tiziano Vecelli), 16, 100
Tunk Mountains, Maine, 71, 94, 100
Turner, Joseph Mallord, 6, 10, 47, 55, 75
"291," 20, 21, 22, 23, 25, 32, 33, 35, 36
Tyrol, The, 23, 26, 27, 45
Tyrrell, Henry, 48n

Union City, New Jersey, 4n, 5, 6, 12, 26, 45
Union Hill, New Jersey, *see* Union City

Van Gogh, Vincent, 30, 99
Van Winkle, John V. S., 4
Venice, Italy, 4, 16, 17, 25
Vermont, state of, 58, 67n
Virginia, state of, 6, 8
Vlaminck, Maurice de, 46
Vollard, Ambroise, 18n

Walden, Lionel, 16
Walker Art Center, 98
Walkowitz, Abraham, 36, 40, 46
Warner, Keith, 37n
Washington, D. C., 28, 98

Wass, Harry, 81-82, 103
Watson, Forbes, 46n
Weber, Max, 25, 46
Wedmore, Sir Frederick, 14n
Weehawken, New Jersey, 3, 4, 7, 8, 10, 37, 41
Westpoint, Maine, 33, 36
Whistler, James A. McNeill, 8, 14, 16, 18, 21, 25, 46
White, Israel L., 23
White Lake, New York, 5, 6
White Mountains, New Hampshire, 61
Whiteface Mountain, see Adirondack Mountains
Whitman, Walt, 39, 53n, 54
Wiese, Lucie, 91n
Wilenski, R. H., 83
Wilmington, Delaware, 5
Wilson, Edmund, 91, 91n
Wiscasset, Maine, 60
Wisconsin, state of, 7
Worcester, Massachusetts, 83n
Wright, S. Macdonald, 40, 46

Yale Art Gallery, 55n

Zayas, Marius, de, 16, 18, 21

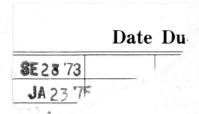